Jesus: The Image of Humanity

Also by Anselm Grün

Images of Jesus

ANSELM GRÜN

Jesus: The Image of Humanity

Luke's Account

Translated by
JOHN BOWDEN

continuum
NEW YORK · LONDON

Continuum

The Tower Building, 11 York Road, London SE1 7NX

370 Lexington Avenue, New York, NY 10017-6503

www.continuumbooks.com

Translated from the German *Jesus – Bild des Menschen: Das Evangelium des Lukas*, published 2001 by Kreuz Verlag GmbH & Co, KG Stuttgart and Zurich

Copyright © 2001 Kreuz Verlag GmbH & Co, KG Stuttgart and Zurich

Translation copyright © John Bowden 2003

First published in English 2003

British Library Cataloguing in Publication Data
A catalogue record for this is available from the British Library

ISBN 08264 68489 (hardback)
08264 68497 (paperback)

Typeset by RefineCatch Ltd, Bungay, Suffolk
Printed and bound in Great Britain by
Biddles Ltd, Guildford and King's Lynn

Contents

CONTENTS

CONTENTS

Introduction

There are countless books which expound the Gospel of Luke or work out individual aspects of its theology. So why this introduction to the Gospel of Luke which is written by someone who is not an exegete?

What I miss in many exegetical works are ways of relating the Gospel to my own spiritual life. So I was very happy to accept an invitation from my publisher to write an introduction to the Gospel of Luke that was easy to understand and would arouse new interest among readers in this marvellous book of the New Testament. The Bible is still the book of all books, the book which nourishes our spiritual life. But my experience is that many Christians find the writings of the New Testament difficult to cope with. They want to encounter Jesus Christ. They ask what this Jesus means for them and how they can live by him and with him. Yet often enough Jesus remains a stranger to them. They listen to the Gospel on Sunday but it doesn't move them. Conversely, I find people who are helped by biblical texts to sort out their lives and to discover a positive way forward for themselves. My concern is to bring out the treasure of the Bible for us today, to help seekers find a new way of approaching the word of God. I want above all to discover Luke's experience of Jesus, so that you as readers and I as an author struggling for the right words can together live by this experience today.

What fascinates me so much about Luke is his attempt to translate the message of Jesus so that it can be understood by the Greek world. Luke was evidently an educated man, well versed in Greek philosophy and literature, but also in contact with the Jewish tradition. So he succeeds in describing Jesus in such a way that both Jews and Greeks learn to understand and love him. Luke personally was deeply moved by Jesus. So he paints an attractive picture of Jesus. He wants to make his readers enthusiastic about this Jesus, above all educated readers who have been shaped by Hellenistic culture. In many respects this Hellenistic culture corresponds to our present-day mentality, which draws on various traditions: from the philosophical thought of the West, but also from religious currents in East and West. Greek philosophy has fascinated me ever since my schooldays. So in my introduction I want above all to examine how what happened to Jesus is translated into the Greek mentality. But I don't want to stop there. For what Luke achieved in his Gospel is the task of theology in any age. It has to express the message of Jesus in such a way that contemporaries feel attracted and moved by it. Luke knew the theology of the Old Testament and he was familiar with Greek philosophy and mythology. He preserves the continuity with Jesus' Jewish roots and the background to his thought. At the same time he opens up Jesus for the Greeks.

In this book I want to take further Luke's attempt to combine the old and the new, to translate what was written then into the present. My concern is to interpret the text in terms of the needs and longings of people who have talked to me about themselves. I want to connect what concerns people today with what it was about Jesus that fascinated Luke, as a man of his time. What moves me in meditating on the Gospel of Luke and the Acts of the Apostles is the question of what drove Luke to set to work with such zeal, investigating all the sources, in order to write the history of Jesus and to depict his effect on the early church. Evidently Luke was personally moved by the message of Jesus. He sees the Spirit of God at work in Jesus and it is also evident in the activity of the apostles. Enthused by this Spirit, he writes his Gospel so that the same Spirit of God may also take hold of his readers and show them the new way to life that Jesus has opened up for us. What I want most is for readers to enjoy meditating on the Gospel of Luke and the Acts of the Apostles. And I want every reader to be guided by Luke to Jesus, to gain new insights into Jesus, and to discover in him the one who gives meaning to our existence, heals our wounds and leads us to true life.

Luke as Author

The tradition of the first centuries sees Luke as a companion of Paul on his missionary journeys. However, present-day exegetes question this, since the theology that Paul presents is substantially different from that of Luke. We cannot be completely certain where Luke came from or what kind of a person he was. But because of his cultivated Greek language we can assume that Luke came from one of the upper levels of society and had a good education in rhetoric and Greek philosophy. At the same time he also had a very good knowledge of the Greek translation of the Bible, the Septuagint. Perhaps he belonged to the circle of the 'godfearers', sympathizers with the Jewish religion. Luke belongs to the second or third generation after the events surrounding the life of Jesus. Tradition thinks that he comes from Antioch, but one modern scholar thinks that he comes from Macedonia, more specifically from Philippi. For in the Acts of the Apostles Luke describes this particular city in great detail, and in so doing betrays his precise knowledge of the place. However, we cannot be certain about this. Jerome reports that Luke wrote his Gospel in Achaea and died in Thebes. That means that he must have lived mainly in Greece. Presumably he wrote his Gospel between 80 and 90. Luke travelled a great deal, and certainly also to Jerusalem, since his descriptions of localities there are also clear. However, he does not seem to have been to Galilee, as the information that he gives about this area is imprecise.

Luke is the only evangelist to speak of himself. In the preface to his Gospel he appears as a historian who carefully investigates all the traditions and from the beginning wants to write everything out accurately. His preface is like the prefaces of books by Hellenistic authors. It is composed in classical Greek. Luke has the ambition of writing a best-seller. His book is intended for the commercial book market. So he dedicates it to a high-ranking and well-to-do figure, the 'most excellent Theophilus'. Theophilus is to act as publisher and distributor for Luke's two books. For from the start Luke conceived his work in two volumes: volume 1 about the events surrounding Jesus, and volume 2 a history of the early church. Luke doesn't call his Jesus book 'gospel', but 'narrative'. He wants to tell the story of Jesus, but not just the individual facts. It was customary in Hellenistic history writing to interpret the facts in presenting them. Indeed for us, facts become meaningful only when they have been interpreted. Luke interpreted the history of Jesus as a history of the salvation and healing of men and women. In the history of Jesus God reveals himself as the God who redeems and saves. What happened then has decisively changed our world. If we grapple with the history of Jesus, it will also transform us.

Luke wants to make his own contribution as an author towards explaining Jesus to people: 'Seeing that many others have undertaken to draw up accounts of the events that have reached their fulfilment among us, as these were handed down to us by those who from the outset were eyewitnesses and ministers of the word, I in my turn, after carefully going over the whole story from the beginning, have decided to write an ordered account for you, Theophilus, so that your Excellency may learn how well founded the teaching is that you have received' (Luke 1.1–4). Luke is clearly dissatisfied with the attempts of his predecessors. They do not tell the beginning of the story or describe its effects in history. They are not composed well, with everything in the right place, and in a style that takes account of the sensibilities of readers. On the one hand Luke puts himself among those who have written before him. On the other hand he dissociates himself from them. Here we have the expression of the self-confidence of a Christian author who is creating his own independent literary work. His work is necessary because he has investigated everything 'carefully' – Greek *akribos*, 'accurately' – from the beginning and sees the internal connection between events. He does not simply relate what has been handed down to him. When he writes he has an overarching idea, a theological conception.

Luke does not present a dogmatic treatise on Jesus but a narrative theology. Narrative theology is user-friendly. It doesn't ask too much of readers by using abstract principles. Readers feel free and can rediscover themselves in the narrative. Luke wants to win over readers by his sensitive account of the actions of Jesus. His book is propaganda for Jesus and his message. In writing it he does not limit himself to the life of Jesus, but also includes the extension of the activity of Jesus in the history of the church. What Jesus said and did is expressed in history. And only when this influence is taken into account do we do justice to the events in Jesus' life. The aim of Luke's work is for readers to recognize how 'well founded' is the teaching that they are given. He wants to give them support and certainty. They are to know what they can build their life on.

After the solemn preface Luke begins his narrative with the sentence, 'And it happened in the days of Herod the king of Judaea' (Luke 1.5). Luke loves the Greek words *kai egeneto*, 'And it happened'. After the marvellous Greek style of the preface, he begins his narrative with a change of style. For the *kai egeneto* – 'and it happened' – is not typically Greek style, but Semitic style – the style of the Septuagint, the Greek translation of the Old Testament. So Luke doesn't want to write profane history but sacred history. And because he is narrating sacred history, he does so in a style which is appropriate to this quite different kind of history. If nowadays someone begins a story with the words 'Once upon a time', we know that it's a fairy tale. So Greeks at that time who were familiar with the Septuagint knew that Luke is now beginning to relate sacred history, the history of God with us men and women. The Greeks called this use of style *mimesis* = imitation. When a Cretan appears in a comedy by a Hellenistic author, he speaks Cretan dialogue. So when Luke imitates the language of the Septuagint, which has a typically Semitic resonance, he is resorting to a typically Hellenistic artifice. By means of it Luke shows that he is doing justice

8

to both Greeks and Jews. He is narrating the history of
Jesus in a language familiar to the Jews. But he dresses up
his narrative in a Greek costume.

2

Luke as Physician and Painter

Luke the physician

In the tradition Luke is regarded as a physician. Some
exegetes emphasize that Luke's language betrays a medical
training. Regardless of whether or not he really was a doctor, the decisive thing is what stands behind this picture
that the tradition has painted of Luke. Evidently Luke was
concerned about the healing of men and women. It
emerges from his Gospel and the Acts of the Apostles that
he does not primarily want to instruct people, but that the
art of a healthy life is important to him. In antiquity doc-
tors saw the art of a healthy life as their most important
task. Luke depicts Jesus as the guide to life, as the one who
introduces us to the art of healthy living, who goes before
us on the way to a fulfilled life. Putting it in modern terms,
we could say that Luke has written a book on 'how faith
helps us to live'.

In his ideas of what a healthy life is Luke is indebted to
the Greek view of human nature. The Greeks thought that
everything should be in moderation. The Greek idea of
the beautiful and good person (Greek *kalos kagathos*) is an

expression of this. Having everything in moderation involves balancing opposites. The basic question for Greeks was how human beings could find their true nature, how they could overcome their inner divisions and find unity with themselves and God. Balancing opposites is a way to achieve this unity. So Luke is fond of including opposites in his account. When he has described one pole of human life, the opposite pole immediately follows. That is evident from the way in which he always puts a woman alongside a man, as in the case of Simeon and Anna, or Simon of Cyrene and the weeping women. A parable involving a man is followed by a parable involving a woman. Luke also shows this in his love of introducing two sisters, two brothers, two pregnant women. He always describes two human poles. Both poles are part of us. Whenever Luke has described a subject that fascinates him, he relativizes it by describing the opposite pole. For example, after talking about love of neighbour (Luke 10.25–37), he immediately relativizes this by talking about love of God (Luke 10.38–42). In this way he preserves us from a one-sided idealism in which we are always in danger of leaping to the opposite pole and thus splitting off important areas of our soul. Luke shows us a balanced way towards becoming human. He teaches us the art of living a full life by consciously perceiving and accepting the polarity of our existence.

The Gospel of Luke is stamped by a positive picture of human nature. Luke is not a moralist nor is he a pessimist. He expects something of men and women. He thinks it important that they should be able to live in their world in a way that accords with their dignity, that they should come into contact with their original beauty and goodness, that they should be able to realize the image of humanity that was so dear to the Greeks. Luke sees Jesus as the one who develops our true image. He refrains from constantly describing men and women as sinners. Human beings have a divine nucleus. But they are alienated from this divine nucleus. So Jesus comes down from heaven to recall them to their divine dignity. Luke's positive picture of human nature would be good for our Christian preaching today. For too long we have thought that we first had to do men and women down so that they accept the grace of God. Luke doesn't adopt such an approach, which ultimately devalues us. He sees human beings as they are, in their dignity, but also with their hurts and wounds. So he depicts Jesus as the true physician who heals our wounds and teaches us the art of healthy living. Jesus is the physician who raises us up to our true dignity when we are turned in on our ourselves and cannot see beyond our narrow horizon.

Luke the painter

The other picture of Jesus that the tradition has handed down to us goes back to Luke as a painter. This too is historically uncertain. Nevertheless, there is a grain of truth in this image. Luke is a gifted writer who has the art of depicting things in such a way that they seem to us to be like a picture. Luke draws a literary portrait of Jesus for us. Some people think that Luke was only a good storyteller, but not a good theologian. I can't share this view. Luke understands the art of telling the story of Jesus in such a way that the whole theology of the incarnation lights up. Luke doesn't need to assert and explain that Jesus is the Son of God. He tells the story of Jesus in such a way that the divine shines out in Jesus. As readers are touched by Jesus, so God dawns on them, and in this way they are drawn into the event of the incarnation. For me that is great theological art.

In Luke's stories the face of God shines out on us in the man Jesus. If we look at this picture, we will be changed by it. Redemption comes about by reading the story. If I read with all my senses, if – as Martin Luther puts it – I creep into the text, I will emerge from the text transformed. I have encountered the figure of Jesus, and this now shapes my figure. The text creates a new reality. Readers don't remain the same. They are recreated by the text. They come into contact with the image of Jesus Christ which forms in them as they read.

Luke was trained in Greek rhetoric. The aim of this rhetoric was to paint pictures before people's eyes. The Roman poet Horace talks of 'painting with words'. Luke is a master of the art of painting a literary portrait of Jesus for us with words. He makes the figure of Jesus visible by describing his gestures and glances. This produces an atmosphere, a sphere of feeling, in which the reader is moved by Jesus. Luke doesn't talk about the incarnation of the love of God but tells a story in which the love of God becomes flesh: the story of the Good Samaritan (Luke 10.30–8). Those who read this story with all their senses alert will feel like the great German poet Rilke when he came to the statue of Laocoön in the Vatican Museums. Rilke stood in front of this fascinating statue and knew that he had to change his life. We can't read a story like this without being moved to become like the picture of Jesus which Luke draws in it.

Let's look at the way in which Luke paints. In his Gospel Jesus illustrates the twofold commandment to love on the one hand by the parable of the Good Samaritan and on the other by his conversation with Mary and Martha (Luke 10.25–42). Luke helps us to understand difficult theological questions by staging impressive scenes, like the virgin birth in which there is a vivid encounter between Mary and the angel and they engage in dialogue (Luke 1.26–38). Luke doesn't go into the question of the mission to the Gentiles with intellectual arguments; he answers it by the specific example of the conversion of Cornelius. He doesn't mention feelings but paints the way in which they are expressed. For example, the unborn John the Baptist leaps in his mother's womb (Luke 1.41), the sinner sheds tears (Luke 7.38), and Jesus bends over Peter's mother-in-law, who is seriously ill (Luke 4.39). Evidently Luke can empathize with any situation. And for every narrative he finds the precise style which will do justice to the events in it. His feelings become visible in language. Luke doesn't identify these feelings. His language expresses the feelings with which he reacts to a particular event or a particular saying of Jesus.

We are indebted to Luke for the finest biblical stories, like the story of the disciples on the road to Emmaus, and for the finest parables (the prodigal son and the dishonest steward). Luke can fascinate the reader. That betrays not only his education but also his sense of beauty and humanity. He has a feeling for people. He loves the people for whom he writes. Through his writing he makes relationships. He works out his two volumes not at the desk, but always in relationship with his readers. As he writes, he has his readers in view and enters into dialogue with them. He wants to win the reader for Jesus – not, however, with empty arguments but with narratives which touch the heart. Only someone who was himself touched by the figure of Jesus can write like that.

However, Luke is concerned not only with the figure of Jesus but ultimately with God's action in Jesus Christ. It is God who is really at work. Luke wants to proclaim God's mighty acts. He doesn't talk in an abstract way about God, but relates God's action with human beings. God becomes visible and can be experienced through his historical activity. Thus in his narratives Luke paints a picture of the invisible God who shows himself to us in his creation and in history.

Language reveals the heart of a person. Luke's language betrays not only the educated person, but also the physician and the painter. It shows us a man who has a heart for his fellow men and women, who wants to win them for life, who wants to show them how they can live a meaningful life here in this world. And it shows an aesthete, a person with a sense of beauty. Luke can tell stories in an exciting way. He has a feeling for composition. Although he has a broad education, he writes simply. He dispenses with the persuasive techniques of Greek rhetoric, which he certainly learned.

Luke adapts his style to the particular situation. He can express Mary's thoughts or worries in motherly words; date the beginnings of John the Baptist in a formal way;

use technical terms in describing a failed fishing trip; depict the transfiguration of Jesus with a sense of mystery; write polemically about Paul's arguments with the Jews in Rome; portray the prayer and attitude of the apostles after the ascension hierarchically, like an icon; describe the encounter with Zacchaeus vividly and movingly and almost naïvely; and relate Paul's dramatic shipwreck as if he were writing a novel. In his missionary speeches Peter is made to speak in the style of the church's preaching; Paul expounds the scriptures in the synagogue with Jewish arguments; and the apostles make speeches in their defence with all the rhetoric of lawyers. Thus the language reveals not only a gifted writer but someone who can empathize with every situation, who feels with the people whom he depicts, who gets involved in life, who is full of longing for a fulfilled life.

I now want to show quite specifically, by means of a few select examples, how Luke also manages to make the story of Jesus speak to our needs and longings.

3

The Stories of Jesus' Childhood

Luke is beyond doubt a prominent representative of what is now called 'narrative theology'. He relates the mystery of Jesus' divine sonship by describing his birth. He does theology by narrating, not by speculating. And Luke is an excellent narrator. That is particularly evident in the stories about Jesus' childhood. We cannot be completely certain precisely what sources he is using here, but we can see how he deals with these sources, how artistically he puts them in order. Luke has dovetailed the birth of Jesus with the story of the birth of John the Baptist to show that Jesus surpasses John, and that John points to Jesus with all his being. Luke contrasts John and Jesus: John preaches judgement, Jesus the good news of the grace of God – of God's winning charm – which fills all those who hear it with joy.

Here Luke has painted two double pictures, rather like a diptych. Here the painter Luke again becomes evident. When he tells a story, pictures emerge. With his pictures Luke refers to previously hidden dimensions of the divine action. The first picture is that of two announcements of births, and the second picture relates the birth of John the

Baptist and the birth of Jesus. Both pictures are followed by meditations on what has happened. After the two announcements of births, Luke tells us about Mary's visit to Elizabeth. The narration of the two births is followed by the testimony of Simeon and Anna about Jesus and the story of the twelve-year-old Jesus in the temple. The mystery of this newborn child shines out in both pictures. Others have developed further the pictures of the birth of Jesus that Luke has created for us. New images of Christmas come into being in every age, interpreting the mystery of the incarnation in their own way. But they all have their basis in the pictures which Luke holds before us in his moving account.

The annunciation by the angel to Mary

Zechariah, the old man and priest, reacts with doubts to the annunciation of the angel Gabriel; Mary, the young woman, the simple girl from Nazareth, believes the angel. Here again we have opposing reactions. Both poles are in us: doubt and faith. Luke invites us, like Mary, to put more trust in the pole of faith. Mary has found grace with God. God is pleased with her and therefore shows her his loving care. What the angel says to Mary also applies to us. God is also well pleased with us. But we do not react. Mary puts her trust in God's grace: 'You see before you the Lord's servant; let it happen to me as you have said' (Luke 1.38). Here Mary also sees herself as a representative of the people of Israel. Whereas Israel has rejected God's will, she will do it on behalf of the people. In this saying Luke shows how much he treasures Mary as a woman. Unlike the man Zechariah she accepts the word of God and trusts it. A woman becomes the representative of the people of Israel. Because she accepts God's word, the people is granted redemption. The action stems from God. But it also depends on a human decision, namely whether she will allow God to act in her. Mary makes room for God's action in her personal life. That has consequences for all of humankind.

In the annunciation scene Mary is described as a virgin. And the birth of Jesus is described as a virgin birth. Exegetes and theologians have had many ideas about this. The motif of a holy man coming into the world through a virgin birth is known both in Jewish circles and in Hellenistic and Egyptian traditions. Philo, the Jewish philosopher, already regards the birth of Isaac as a virgin birth, and he speaks of the ecstatic union of the soul with God. In the Egyptian cult of the sun the birth of the sun was celebrated in the night of 24/25 December. At that time the community exclaimed, 'The virgin has given birth, the light increases.' People at that time thought that the Egyptian king had been fathered by God. All these elements of the Egyptian cult of the sun and Hellenistic notions of divine procreation were already widespread in Judaism. Thus Luke has on the one hand used Jewish traditions, and on the other has also responded to the longings of the Greeks. With his narrative of the annunciation he can explain the virginity of the mother of the messiah, his greatness and his divine sonship, his eternal rule and his procreation through the Holy Spirit. Just as the winter solstice follows the summer solstice after six months, so Jesus is born six months after John. With him the sun of the divine grace shines out brightly in the chill of our world. At that time, in a consummate way, Luke was already carrying on the dialogue with other religions that many theologians are calling for today. He has taken up the various religious currents, and against this background formulated the mystery of Jesus in such a way that men and women from every religious culture could understand what God has given them in Jesus.

But Luke combines these mythological motifs with the human motif of the trusting faith that he describes in Mary. Mary becomes the original and the model and the example of faith. Mary listens to the angel. Certainly she is terrified when the angel addresses her. However, she does not disguise this, but thinks about what the angel really wants to tell her. The angel proclaims to her that she will conceive a son, who will be called 'son of the Most High' (1.32). In Hellenistic Judaism 'Most High' is a popular designation for God. The angel tells Mary how the conception will take place: 'The Holy Spirit will come upon you, and the power of the Most High will overshadow you' (Luke 1.35). The Holy Spirit himself will impregnate the virgin. That not only explains the virgin birth of Jesus but is also an image for our life. The most precious fruit that we can bear doesn't come from ourselves, nor does it come from fertilization by other human beings; it is brought about by the Holy Spirit. Mary, the woman who believes, is here a model for Christians. God also wants to create new things in us through his Holy Spirit. We mustn't have too low an opinion of ourselves. Like Mary, we must trust that God will do great things in us and is able to work through us. 'For nothing is impossible to God' (Luke 1.37).

True faith consists in our setting no limits to God. God is not impossible. God chooses the virgin Mary, an insignificant girl from Nazareth, to make the impossible possible in this world. He also chooses us, in our weakness and limitations, to perfect his work of salvation and healing in this world through us. Christ also wants to take shape in us. However, the presupposition for this is that, like Mary, we say, 'You see before you the Lord's servant; let it happen to me as you have said' (Luke 1.38).

The meeting between Mary and Elizabeth

Before Luke describes the birth of John and the birth of Jesus, he tells us the beautiful story of Mary's meeting with Elizabeth. By means of this story, on the one hand he links the birth of John with the birth of Jesus, and on the other he interprets the event for us. Mary is the woman who is blessed more than all other women. For she bears the Lord himself within her. Luke tells us the story of a marvellous meeting. A twelve- or fourteen-year-old girl gets up and rushes through the hills. Normally this journey took four days. Mary must have been a self-confident woman to make it by herself. The experience of God in the scene of the annunciation has got her moving. And Elizabeth is also made to move. When Mary greets her, the child in her womb jumps. She comes into contact with her fertility, with the new thing that is growing in her. And she is filled with the Holy Spirit. She becomes a prophetess who in Mary recognizes the mystery of her motherhood. This marvellous story isn't just about what happened at that time. The scene is rather the model for any deep human encounter. Every encounter is about discovering the mystery of Christ in the other. We all bear Christ in ourselves. When we understand that, then the child in us jumps. We discover the mystery of the other and our own mystery. We come into contact with the child in us. For such a meeting to become possible, like Mary we must get up and set out on the way. We must stand on our own feet if we are to reach the other. And we must go over the hills, the mountains of inhibitions and prejudices, to see others as they are.

Elizabeth praises Mary for having believed that fulfilment will come through what the Lord has promised her. This is the only time in his Gospel that Luke uses the word *teleiosis*, fulfilment. The birth of Jesus is the fulfilment of all the promises that God ever made in the Old Testament. It sums up all that God has promised men and women. In Jesus God shows that he will rescue his people from all tribulation, that he will show them the way of life, that he will redeem them from captivity and heal all their wounds. This is not a matter of relating individual promises to the birth of Jesus but of seeing in Jesus the fulfilment of the whole of holy scripture. Elizabeth sees Mary as the believer who is also the model for our faith. God will also fulfil in us what he has promised us. He will also bring about great things in us, if like Mary we trust his word.

Mary answers the beatitude with a song of praise which Luke formulates in such a way that it can also become our song. In the Magnificat Mary interprets the event that she has experienced in the annunciation and that will be fulfilled in the birth of Jesus. Here Mary is the representative of Israel, but also the voice of all the poor and those without rights, who gain their rights through the birth of Jesus. In Jesus' birth God casts down the mighty from their thrones, and the poor are raised up. Liberation theology has rediscovered the Magnificat today as the song of hope of the poor. Feminist theologians see it as a song of liberation for women. Both movements take up important concerns of the evangelist. For Luke is both the advocate of the poor and the advocate of women. We can all sing this marvellous song for ourselves and in so doing praise the God who also looks upon the insignificant and has done great things through them. This song tells how God shakes up all our criteria by exalting what is lowly in us and satisfying what is hungry in us.

The birth of Jesus

There cannot be anyone who isn't touched by the story of Jesus' birth as Luke tells it for us. Luke has artistically woven three events together: the census, the birth of Jesus and the proclamation of the birth to the shepherds. Exegetes today are agreed that there never was a tax assessment covering all the empire, but only in individual regions. Luke doesn't simply report the historical facts but interprets them. He sets the birth of Jesus in the political world of the emperor Augustus to show that Jesus is the true king of peace; that it is not Augustus who brings salvation, as some of his inscriptions claim, but Jesus, born a poor child in a stable. This birth in an insignificant corner of Palestine is healing for the whole world. Jesus is the true saviour and lord. He is the one who brings true peace, not Augustus, who had himself celebrated as the emperor of peace. With his story Luke is criticizing the ideology of imperial rule and at the same time also the political theology of the Zealots, who rebelled against the census. Mary and Joseph obey the emperor's command. Conditions aren't changed by violence and external force, but from within. In Jesus God has intervened in this history. The peace which appears in history with Jesus has historical and political effects. Luke thinks that Christians are to bring the peace of Christ to the whole world. Through Christians, the story of Jesus is to have a healing effect on world history and to bring peace. The peace of God becomes visible in the history of Jesus and through him will permeate the whole of world history.

Mary and Joseph set off for Bethlehem. 'While they were there, the time came for her to have her child, and she gave birth to a son, her firstborn. She wrapped him in swaddling clothes and laid him in a manger because there was no room for them at the inn' (Luke 2.6f.). The inn in which there is no room for the couple is a room in a private house in which travellers could usually spend the night. But there was no longer any room in the house. So Joseph and Mary had to go into the cave under the house where a food trough had been hewn in the wall. The room in which Jesus is born is a room of the utmost poverty. Luke sees the fulfilment of God's promises to his people in this birth. That becomes evident in the scene with the shepherds. Israel understands itself as a shepherd people. The message of the birth of Jesus is first proclaimed to the shepherds as representatives of the poor of the people. But a Greek motif is certainly also in play here. The Greeks tell of the discovery of a royal infant by shepherds. Luke narrates his

Gospel in such a way that it is good news for both Jews and Greeks, a message which speaks to their intellectual horizons and fulfils their deepest longings. An angel comes to the shepherds, and with the angel God's glory appears and shines on the shepherds. The night, the darkness of the human heart, is transformed by God's light. The angel proclaims great joy to the shepherds. Here Luke uses the Greek word *euangelizomai*. It is a word which designates the announcements of the emperor but at the same time also has its roots in the Old Testament. With this word God gives his message to humankind. Luke uses every word deliberately. He is a master of the art of addressing both the Jews and the Greeks. For the Jews it becomes clear that the Old Testament promises are being fulfilled in the birth of Jesus. For the Greeks the word has an anti-imperial ring. The proclamation of the birth of Jesus brings people true joy, not the promises of the emperor.

The content of the angel's proclamation is: 'Today in the town of David a saviour has been born to you; he is the messiah, the lord' (Luke 2.11). Here Luke uses three terms to explain the mystery of Jesus. And these are terms that again speak equally to Jews and Greeks. In the Septuagint the word *soter* = 'saviour' denotes the activity of God. In the Graeco-Roman world emperors, philosophers and physicians are called saviour. The emperor Augustus was called saviour. But Jesus surpasses all these human saviours. He is the messiah, God's anointed. The true saviour is the messiah who comes from Judaism. This messiah fulfils God's promises. He frees his people from oppression and slavery. Here the Jewish term messiah stands between the two Greek titles 'saviour' and 'lord'.

Kyrios = 'lord' is a term which the Greeks used for the emperor. In the Septuagint God is the real Lord. Jesus both comes from God and is God's son. But at the same time he is the lord, who brings peace and salvation to the whole world, more permanently than any emperor can. Luke describes the mystery of the incarnation of God in Jesus Christ by artistically combining these three terms. He does not speculate on them, but indicates who this Jesus is through a narrative. We prefer a story to the often incomprehensible theological discussions about the divine sonship of Jesus that we hear. In this moving story of the birth of Jesus we get some inkling of the mystery of this man. He is fully man, but he comes from God. He is the saviour for whom the whole world longs. In this narrative Luke brings together heaven and earth, human longing and divine action. By the way in which Luke tells of the birth of Jesus he brings about in us the joy that the angel proclaims. The divine becomes visible and tangible through human words.

Here the word 'today' appears for the first time. Luke will use it seven times in his Gospel. What happened then happens for us today when we read Luke's story. 'Today' we take part in the drama that Luke describes for us. We look upon what is painted in words before our eyes. And by looking we become one with what we look at. We become eyewitnesses to the event, spectators at the divine drama, when the words are proclaimed to us in the liturgy and when in the liturgy we take part in the event in such a way that by looking and in acting we are transformed and go home different people. Luke says his 'today' to all our longings. Today what the shepherds once experienced will happen to us. Today all our longings will be fulfilled.

A whole host of angels appears alongside the angel who makes the proclamation, praising God and singing, 'Glory to God in the highest heaven, and on earth peace for those he favours' (Luke 2.14). Heaven and earth are interwoven through the birth of Jesus. God's glory appears on high. And down below, on earth, God's peace appears in Jesus. It's a paradox: through the birth of a child in the stable God's glory shines out in heaven before the angels. The reflection of God's glory on earth is peace. *Eirene* = 'peace' here doesn't mean just the removal of war and conflict, but the salvation that God brings about. The Hebrew word *shalom* means the state of humankind as it really should be. In the birth of Jesus God restores human beings to the state that he really intended. The Greek word *eirene* means rest, the rest of the soul. When God becomes man, human beings find rest in their restless hearts. Their longings are fulfilled. And *eirene* is also connected with harmony. Everything is in tune. In the birth of Jesus God and human beings, heaven and earth, are in tune. There is harmony between God and humankind, between spirit and matter, between angels and human beings. This peace, rest, harmony are promised to men and women with whom God is well pleased. *Eudokia* means God's favour, God's loving care for human beings. The word expresses divine goodwill towards men and women; it conveys Luke's image of God, with its deeply emotional stamp. God has shown humankind his love in the birth of Jesus. His act of love calls for a reciprocal act of love in human beings. *Eudokia* expresses the fact that God is always in relationship with human beings and wants to deepen this relationship through the birth of his son.

Hearing the angels' song of praise, the shepherds set out to see the child in the manger. The shepherds and Mary are models for the faith with which we are to respond to God's visit to humankind in the birth of Jesus. The shepherds see what the angel has promised them. And they interpret what they see through the word that they have heard. Mary keeps these sayings in her heart; she interprets them in order to understand what has happened. However, this is no intellectual understanding but a movement of the divine word in her heart, a clear and correct interpretation of the divine action at the level of feeling. We likewise are to consider the story of the birth of Jesus in our hearts. We are to ponder it until our feelings fall into line with the mystery of the divine love that has broken into history in the birth of Jesus and has appeared visibly for all of us.

Simeon and Anna

However, the shepherds and Mary are not the only model for accepting Jesus Christ the Son of God in faith. Luke the narrator takes over yet another important motif that was popular both among the Greeks and among the Jews: the old person who still has a special experience. Luke loves meetings between human beings that are initiated by God himself. The mystery of God for human beings can be experienced in such encounters. For Luke, the Greek, these are always meetings with men and women. Both together embrace the event and in so doing recognize the activity of God. But this story doesn't just express the polarity of man and woman. It also opposes law and gospel, joy and sorrow, being raised up and the pain that Jesus will cause his mother. Mary doesn't expect a world that has been healed. Mingled with the joy over her son, God's anointed, is pain over the fate that he will suffer. Here Luke brings out the contradictions in our own soul. We too experience God as the one who delights our hearts, but also as the incomprehensible God, the God who provokes conflict in us and expects us to make a painful change.

Mary and Joseph fulfil the law of Moses by bringing the child to Jerusalem in order to dedicate him to the Lord. But the law is merely the transition to the grace of God which has appeared in Jesus. While they are performing the prescribed rite they have a surprise: they meet Simeon and Anna. Luke doesn't speculate on the relationship between law and grace, but he expresses it through his narrative. This is a story that has touched many hearts. Origen alone was so fascinated by this text that he gave four sermons on it. Luke doesn't just relate the mystery of Jesus that Simeon celebrates in his song of praise. He also presents Simeon as a model. Simeon is the image of the person who can look back gratefully on his life in the face of death. For when we Christians die we may confess, 'Lord, now let your servant depart in peace, as you have promised. For my eyes have seen the salvation that you have prepared before all peoples' (Luke 2.29ff.). After the hymn Luke depicts the conflict in Simeon's heart, which is also in all our hearts. For us Jesus is peace and light, but also a sword and suffering. Mary is pierced by a sword. She will take part in the suffering of Jesus. Jesus doesn't just bring salvation but also judgement. Through him the thoughts of men and women are made manifest. It becomes clear how human beings are shut off from God. In this tension between light and suffering Luke indicates that he is not just writing a simple narrative but a tragedy like a Greek tragedy, which also sets out to address and to purge people's feelings by different emotions.

Anna appears alongside Simeon. Whereas Simeon is described as a pious and just man, Anna is called a prophetess. The man alone never represents faith as Luke understands it. A woman always has to be set against him to express the other aspect of the acceptance of Jesus in faith. Luke had described the man as just and pious. He illuminates the woman's character by describing the history of her life and her present action. This is the art of the writer who alternates between description and narration. Anna has lived through all three stages of womanhood: virginity, marriage and widowhood. She is a woman who prays. She is constantly in the temple. And she is a prophetess. She sees more deeply. She sees what God is doing in Jesus. In Jesus the redemption for which pious Israelites long becomes a reality for all men and women. They are freed from their captivity, freed from their alienation. They become free, just as God had intended when he created them.

After the encounter with Simeon and Anna, Mary and Joseph return home from Jerusalem, to everyday life in Nazareth. 'The child grew and became strong: God filled him with wisdom, and his grace rested on him' (Luke 2.40). Luke loves the word *charis* = 'grace'. He uses the word in the Greek sense: something that brings joy. *Charis* denotes

attractiveness, grace, a quality that gives pleasure, something associated with elegance and beauty. In this sense
charis expresses a typically Greek feeling. As a growing
child Jesus gives pleasure by his attractive nature, his
beauty and charm.

But after this ideal picture of the adolescent Jesus Luke
immediately introduces the opposite pole. Jesus is not a
loving and dutiful child. In the narrative about the twelve-
year-old Jesus in the temple Luke depicts the first family
conflict. Jesus becomes independent. He doesn't return to
Jerusalem with his parents. When they find him in the
temple after three days of vain searching, he is sitting in
the midst of the teachers, listening to them and asking
them questions (Luke 2.46). Mary's words are full of
reproach, and convey the pain that her son has caused her:
'My child, why have you done this to us? See how worried
your father and I have been, looking for you' (Luke 2.48).
Jesus' reply remains incomprehensible to his parents. Jesus
calls God his Father. He belongs to God, not to his parents.
Here for the first time in the Gospel of Luke Jesus speaks
of God as his Father. His parents have to accept that their
son is a stranger. What Luke depicts here is not a tranquil
family, but a family with the kind of conflicts that we
all know: the suffering caused by the recognition that
children are different, the pain in letting go of a child, a
failure to understand his or her ways. Yet this conflict
typical of puberty is again followed by the description of
an ideal: 'And Jesus increased in wisdom, in stature and in
favour with God and with people' (Luke 2.52). Ideal and
reality alternate. Both poles belong to Jesus, and both poles
also belong to us. Only in the tension between intimacy

and detachment, between understanding and failure to understand, between fellowship and alienation, do we grow into a form which pleases God and corresponds to our inner beauty (*charis*).

The narrative with which Luke brings the story of Jesus before our eyes is an artistic one. In the few remarks that I have made about it I want to arouse the curiosity of readers about the gifted writer Luke who addresses Jewish and Greek readers in the same way, who beyond all religious and cultural traditions touches the hearts of men and women directly with his words, and arouses in them a sense of the mystery of God. Luke never lays things on too thick. He has a fine sense of the particular situation that he is depicting. And he relates events in such a way that we can sense their deeper meaning. He offers us images in a restrained and cautious way, so that we see through them to the depths of the divine mystery. We will never grow tired of looking at these pictures. In every situation new facets of the divine love will dawn on us if we listen to the narrative of the birth and childhood of Jesus.

It is not just the writer's art that moves Luke to keep setting two pairs and two poles opposite each other. We have Jesus and John, Mary and Elizabeth. We have Mary and Joseph, Mary and the shepherds, and finally Simeon and Anna. We have the fulfilling of the emperor's command and the uncalled-for event of the grace of God, the legally prescribed rite of purification and the radiance of the gospel in Simeon's promise. We have Jesus the salvation of all peoples and at the same time the cause of conflict among them. This polarity gives Luke's narrative its tension. But we can also interpret this narrative skill in terms of depth psychology. Then Luke shows that we must always combine two poles in ourselves, so that something new can come to birth and Christ can grow in us. We must combine *anima* and *animus*, the male and the female in us, the old and the young, law and grace, assent and contradiction. Like Mary we must ponder all these opposites in our hearts, accept them and understand them. Then Christ will become our salvation; then he will heal our divisions and put us right, shape us as people who correspond to God's original image, people who are just and upright.

4

Sickness and Healing in Luke

Tradition also saw Luke as a physician because he is a master of medical language. In no other Gospel do the words *iaomai* = 'heal' and *therapeuein* = 'cure' appear as frequently as they do in Luke. Christ is the one who brings salvation to men and women, who heals their wounds. Here Luke develops his understanding of sickness and healing in the light of the Greek view of human nature. For the Greeks the ideal of human nature was the *kalos kagathos* = the beautiful and good person. Health was an expression of beauty and goodness. A healthy soul lives in a healthy body (*mens sana in corpore sano*). According to Plato, the healthy person is someone whose body and all parts of whose soul live together in harmony. Health also includes morality. And it requires moderation in all things. Those who are centred only on their health, like athletes, aren't truly healthy. For a person to be healthy, everything must be in the right proportion. When people are sick, their dignity is infringed and the harmony of the parts of their souls is destroyed. So health is the restoration of human dignity and harmony. That becomes clear when we interpret the two stories of healings that only Luke relates:

the healing of the woman bent double and the healing of the man with dropsy. Both healings take place on the sabbath. The sabbath is the day on which God rested from his works and saw that the creation was good. For Luke, healing is restoration of the good creation. When Jesus heals a person he completes the work of the Father; he shows how human beings were intended from God's hand. The mastery of Luke the author and theologian becomes evident in this combination of the Greek picture of human nature with the biblical notion of the original beauty and goodness of creation. He proclaims his message in such a way that both Jews and Greeks understand it and love it in the same way. And at the same time he also offers us today a view of sickness and healing that we understand. Psychology has rediscovered the connection between body and soul. Many illnesses are psychosomatic. They affect the body and the soul. Healing never affects only the body; it also restores the soul. It is always about the whole person, about its again assuming the form that it has received from God. Through sickness our original undamaged form is deformed. Healing is reshaping, orientation on what is original and authentic in human beings.

The healing of the woman bent double

Jesus teaches in a synagogue: 'And there before him was a woman who for eighteen years had been possessed by a spirit of sickness; she was bent double and quite unable to stand upright. When Jesus saw her he called her over and said, "Woman, you are freed from your disability," and he laid his hands on her. And at once she straightened up, and she glorified God' (Luke 13.11–13). The strange expression 'spirit of sickness' probably means that the sickness was not purely physical, but expresses a basic psychological attitude. The bodily illness indicates the spirit that controls the woman. It is a spirit which burdens her, bends her double and blocks her. The woman is bent over because she is oppressed with the burden of life, because she droops in a resigned way. She goes around sorry and depressed. Those who are bent over in this way become depressive. Their breathing gets shallow, and their faces lose their original beauty. The bent back could also point to feelings which aren't accepted. Some people carry a whole rucksack of completely repressed feelings around with them. They misuse their backs as places on to which they offload their suppressed emotions. They prefer to suffer from back pains than to come into contact with their feelings.

Perhaps the woman has also been oppressed. Perhaps her backbone has been broken. She is incapable of standing up of her own accord. She can't walk upright. She can't stand by herself. The Greek word *panteles* = 'complete, absolute, for ever', indicates that the sickness is incurable, that this woman can never straighten herself out again. She can never stand upright again. She is cut off from her contact with God. She directs her gaze only to the ground, below. She has a narrow horizon and she has lost her human dignity, her breadth and freedom. And has done for eighteen years. If we understand eighteen as a symbolic figure, we could say that ten is the number of totality, of a person's integrity. The woman has lost her totality, her original beauty and goodness. Eight is the number of eternity and infinity. The fonts in early churches are octagonal. They show that in baptism the Christian takes part in the eternal life of God. The woman who has been sick for eighteen years has lost her contact with God. She can no longer look up to God. Her gaze is obscured.

Luke sees in this woman bent double the image of the oppressed person who is broken and whose dignity has been infringed. And he shows us how Jesus can heal not only this woman but also us today. Jesus notices this woman. He looks at her and thus gives her some respect. Jesus isn't indifferent to human misery. He turns to the woman. Luke doesn't mention Jesus' feeling of pity, but he expresses Jesus' feelings through the narrative. His action shows how tenderly and lovingly he deals with the woman. Having perceived the woman's distress and oppression, he speaks to her. The Greek word *prosphono* = 'address, call by name' expresses the relationship which Jesus restores to the woman. He speaks to her. His words are addressed to her. He lures her out of the isolation into which she has withdrawn, probably out of a sense of shame when in the company of healthy people. The woman allows Jesus to get her moving. Jesus is evidently capable of addressing people in such a way that he touches and moves them. When the woman appears before him he says to her, 'Woman, you are freed from your illness.' He promises her healing and liberation. In the presence of Jesus people can no longer be bound; they become free and find their dignity. The upright man Jesus sets the oppressed woman upright and restores her to her unique and divine dignity. Jesus expresses this by laying his hands on her. In the Gospel of Luke and the Acts of the Apostles the laying on of hands either communicates healing or invokes the Holy Spirit. The two go together. By the laying on of hands God's Holy Spirit streams into the woman. The Holy Spirit is always also a spirit of healing. And it embodies the power of God which drives out the woman's weakness. The disciples, too, are to lay their hands on people and in this way to communicate God's healing power to them, thus freeing them from the power of Satan. Men and women are no longer to be shaped by their old patterns of life but by the healing and liberating power of God, by the love of God which streams to them in Jesus and makes them what God originally meant them to be. The moment Jesus touches the woman, she stands upright. She stands upright and praises God. Now the eighteen have been achieved. She has become whole, and she has again made contact with God. The Greek word for 'raise up' = *anortho* is also used for the 'rebuilding' of a house. Jesus is the one who raises people up again, who restores them to their original beauty, who builds the houses of their lives in such a way that God may dwell in them with his glory.

The ruler of the synagogue is annoyed at the healing of the woman bent double. One shouldn't work on the sabbath. He interprets the healing of the woman as human work. Jesus sees it as the action of God. The ruler of the synagogue is exaggerating in his interpretation of the law. The law is more important than human beings. Jesus robs his rigid attitude of its force by referring to the animals that are released from the manger and taken for a drink. If oxen and asses are released, it is also permissible to set human beings free from their fetters. For Luke, God is above all the redeemer, the one who redeems his people from slavery, who restores men and women to the state in which God created them. The sabbath recalls the creation. On the seventh day God rests from his creation. Then he contemplates it in its splendour. For Luke, the best way of celebrating the sabbath is to raise up men and women to their original form, to delight in the divine dignity and to praise God, the creator of human dignity. The reaction of the people is joy 'at all the great deeds that he did' (Luke 13.17). People always react joyfully to Jesus' offer of redemption. Jesus doesn't talk about joy; his action sparks off joy among people. Luke relates the healing of the woman bent double in such a way that those who get fully caught up with this text will go their way more upright. The liberation depicted in the text will spill over to readers and hearers, so that they can delight in their divine dignity and go home upright.

The healing of the man with dropsy

The second healing which can only be found in Luke also occurs on the sabbath: the healing of the man with dropsy (Luke 14.1–6). Here the healing is described only briefly. The decisive notion is that healing is not a human work but the action of God. Dropsy is mentioned time and again by Greek physicians. The famous physician Galen alone speaks of dropsy 48 times and gives various recipes for healing it. Dropsy shows itself in swellings, above all of the stomach. It weakens the heart and can lead to sudden death. In the Jewish tradition dropsy is usually regarded as a consequence of sexual deviation, calumniation and idolatry (the golden calf). The rabbinic view is that human beings are composed of water and blood, and those who lose their equilibrium by departing from virtue contract either dropsy or leprosy, the latter when blood gets the upper hand. Today we would say that when people lose their sense of moderation, when they ask too much of themselves, their bodies also react chaotically. The various fluids get out of order. So here again it is a matter of moderation. People are healthy if they live in accordance with their nature. When they lose this moderation they fall sick. Healing means getting things back in proportion and living accordingly.

Jesus asks the teachers of the law and the Pharisees, 'Is it permissible to heal on the sabbath or not?' With this question Jesus focuses on the correct interpretation of the sabbath and healing. What is the sabbath about? And in what does healing consist? For Jesus the sabbath is a day on which works are done in accordance with the image of God's works. And healing is the work of God, not human work. When the Pharisees are silent in response to Jesus' question, he acts as God means him to: 'He took the man and cured him and sent him away' (Luke 14.4). Jesus takes the hand of the sick man in order to help him. And then Luke uses the word which is essential to Jesus' healing work: *iasato* = 'he healed'. Luke uses this word fifteen times. Jesus is the doctor who restores people to what they are meant to be by God. He is the therapist who restores moderation to people who have lost their equilibrium. The third word used to describe the healing is *apolyo* = 'liberate, loose, release'. Luke has already used this word in the healing of the woman bent double. Healing is a matter of liberating human beings, loosing them from the bonds of sickness and from the fetters of the demons. Here the word means 'let go'. Jesus lets go of the sick person. Now he can go his own way. But Luke loves ambiguous words. For him the meanings 'loose' and 'liberate' are certainly also present. The healed person is always also the liberated person who is loosed from all blockages and redeemed. Sickness is like being bound. Any bond to a pattern of life, a habit, an obsession, even any bond to other people, sparks off a negative energy in us, against ourselves and the other. Healing means liberation from all bonds and thus the dissolving of inner negativity. This freedom from being bound enables us to make good relationships, friendships. The capacity for relationship, the capacity for having good friends, is an essential part of health. And for the Greeks this capacity for friendship in particular is essential for the image of the beautiful and good person.

God has created people free and upright. So Jesus restores them on the sabbath and in this way shows how God means people to be. Luke combines a theology of creation with a theology of redemption. Redemption means showing creation in its true splendour. Human beings have been created good by God. But they have fallen sick, fettered to their passions, bound to their needs. Jesus liberates people and raises them up again. He makes them whole and healthy, beautiful and good. When Jesus heals people, he restores them to the state in which God created them in their original beauty and their original goodness. So the most important healings of Jesus in Luke take place on the sabbath, when God rested from his creation. But there is yet another reason why Luke puts these sabbath healings at the centre of his theology of healing. On Sunday Christians come together to break bread with one another, and in worship to celebrate the one who at that time in history healed people and raised them up. The healing activity of Jesus is made present in the liturgy. So Luke has people reacting to the healing of the paralysed man with the words, 'We have seen incredible things today' (Luke 5.26). What happened then, happens 'today' when Christians meet for Sunday worship. The eucharist is the place of healing. And the reading, the meditation on the biblical narrative, can become the place at which we as readers are taken up into the drama of healing that Luke presents to us with his words.

Jesus' mission as a physician

Luke also shows how he understands the healing of the sick in his depiction of the first appearance of Jesus. Before Luke reports the first healing miracle, he relates the scene in the synagogue of Nazareth. Luke heightens his hearers' tension by depicting at length how Jesus stands up, is given the book, opens it and finds in it the passage with the words of the prophet Isaiah: 'The spirit of the Lord is on me; for he has anointed me, to bring the good news to the poor. He has sent me to proclaim liberty to captives, sight to the blind, to let the oppressed go free, to proclaim a year of grace from the Lord' (Luke 4.18f.).

Jesus is formulating his own programme in these words of the prophet Isaiah. It is interesting that here Luke is mixing two texts, the messianic text from Isaiah 61.1f. and the statement 'to let the oppressed go free' from Isaiah 58.6.

This text speaks of proper fasts, of the fasting that God loves.

It is no coincidence that Luke has put things together like this. Jesus is fulfilling the tasks of the messiah. He is the one who pleases God in his piety. And with this combination of the two texts Luke is indicating that like the disciples of Jesus we have the task of letting the oppressed go free, of smoothing the way to freedom for those who are hurt, beaten, oppressed, worn out.

Jesus understands himself to be someone who is filled with the spirit of God. And he sees his task as proclaiming the good news to the poor. These poor are on the one side the economically poor and those without social rights, and on the other the prisoners, the blind and the oppressed. Luke understands Jesus' healing of people as liberation from the chains that hold them prisoner. Here Luke introduces only the blind as an example of the healing of the sick. Jesus wants to make these people see again, or as it says literally, to give them 'sight'. Those who have closed their eyes to reality are to open their eyes again. With their eyes they are to discover the beauty of the world. It is remarkable that here Luke emphasizes only seeing. However, for the Greek, sight is the most important sense. For the Greeks God is the one who is seen (the Greek word for God, *theos*, comes from *theastai* = 'to be seen'; God comes from being seen). People experience their dignity in seeing. But often enough their sight is blurred. They see reality through the misty glass of their projections or their neurotic patterns. Their view is distorted by their illusions about the world. When they are capable of seeing what is, of looking up in order to look around freely, they are really human.

Jesus sums up his mission in the proclamation of the year of grace. The year of grace is the Jewish year of jubilee. In this year, which took place every 50 years, the Israelites were to release all slaves, to remit all debts and to allow the fields to lie fallow. These are marvellous images of the activity of Jesus. Where Jesus appears, slaves are set free; enslaved people can break out of the inner prison of their anxiety and alien domination and rediscover their human dignity. Luke depicts the freeing of slaves during the first healing, which he attaches directly to the narrative of the appearance of Jesus in the synagogue at Nazareth. In it he relates how a man sat in the synagogue of Capernaum 'who was possessed by the spirit of an unclean demon' (Luke 4.31). Demons stand for people being dominated by suffering, oppression, bullying, neuroses, compulsive behaviour, obsessions. They can be taken over by such spirits to such a degree that they can no longer be themselves; they lose their identity and their personality and are completely alienated from themselves and their environment. Their thought is disturbed by prejudices, bitterness, anxiety and jealousy. For Luke, healing means that people can see clearly again, that they are freed from all the demons that enslave them.

Where Jesus proclaims his good news of the nearness of the gracious God, people feel free from their guilt. Sinners are confident enough to approach Jesus and ask him for forgiveness. Then despite their guilt they experience that they are unconditionally accepted. Luke instils this experience in his readers by the marvellous story of the woman who was a sinner. She dares to enter the house of the Pharisee in order to anoint Jesus' feet (Luke 7.36–50).

Where Jesus appears, space is opened up in which people can breathe again. That is probably the significance of the image of fields lying fallow. Jesus conveys to people that they needn't work all the time; sometimes they can allow the field of their soul to lie fallow and trust that God will sow his good seed in them. Then the field will bring forth fruit one hundredfold by the grace of God.

After the expulsion of the demons in 4.33–7, Luke describes how Jesus heals Peter's mother-in-law. He bends over her in order to be near to her, to communicate something of his spirit to her. In this gesture Luke describes the tenderness with which Jesus approaches the sick woman. And Jesus combines his gesture with a word. He rebukes the fever. He personifies the fever that is dominating the woman and commands it to leave the woman. The woman is immediately healed. She gets up and serves Jesus. After the healing of a man Luke immediately relates the healing of a woman. For him it is always important that men and women appear side by side on equal terms. He has already shown this in Jesus' inaugural speech in Nazareth, where he refers to Naaman the Syrian and the widow of Zarephath as examples of people who experienced healing through the prophets.

Then Luke relates the activity of Jesus as a physician. The gracious messiah takes on the role of the Hellenistic physician. Jesus is described in such a way that the Greeks learn to understand him and love him. He heals people of their sickness; he lays hands on them and communicates God's spirit and power to them, and this restores them and gives them back their original form. However, Jesus doesn't just heal through contact, but also through his word, through his teaching, in which he teaches people the 'art of healthy living' after the fashion of Greek medicine. Sometimes he has to prescribe bitter medicine, like the physician whom Socrates portrays in his dialogue called *Gorgias*, medicine which at first glance doesn't suit them. For Luke the words of Jesus are words which lead people to their salvation, which bring them to their true being. Jesus as physician and therapist is a picture of Jesus which speaks to people today. They long for healing.

Self-help books are extremely popular today. And the market for cures which promise to heal our ailments is booming. Luke shows us Jesus as a therapist whose methods are as modern today as they were then. And he calls on us Christians, in the power of the Spirit in which Jesus is steeped, also to heal the sick today and to raise up those who are bowed down.

5

Parables of Jesus

Jesus isn't just a therapist but also a gifted teller of parables. In the parables he can describe his view of God and human beings most clearly. Parables have the function of getting people out of where they are. In the parables Jesus often relates everyday situations in which people can find themselves. Or he depicts agricultural work. Evidently Jesus could speak about the specific features of the lives of men and women in such a way that he captivated his hearers. Jesus expresses the feelings of his audience and puts them under his spell. But then all at once he opens their eyes to God. All at once it dawns on them, 'God is like that. That is how God acts with us.' Jesus doesn't talk about God in an abstract way. He begins with people. He talks about people and their everyday life in such a way that his hearers can understand who God is and how God acts. The parables are always about transforming the audience and their perceptions and introducing them to a new picture of God and their fellow human beings. In the parables we encounter Jesus' authentically personal way of talking about God. Luke has fashioned the parables which Jesus told so artistically that not only were the Greeks attracted by them; we too are moved by them in our hearts.

In the parables Jesus doesn't speak only of God and of human beings in their relationship to God. The parables are also authentic self-portraits of Jesus. In his parables Jesus portrayed himself – and it is no coincidence that Luke, who is celebrated in iconography as a painter, has copied these portraits most successfully. So in the parables we encounter the man Jesus with his personal attractiveness, with his distinctive way of thinking and speaking. In the parables Jesus doesn't just speak of the kingdom of God but makes that kingdom present. The kingdom of God comes to us in the words of Jesus; it can be experienced; it is tangible. Heaven opens above us and we understand that God is acting in us now. At this moment God becomes flesh. God becomes language. God expresses himself in language, effective language which brings God's kingdom to hearers and readers. The kingdom of God is made reality through the image of the parables.

Luke has handed down to us the most beautiful parable of all, one that has been repeated and interpreted in literature time and again, more often than any other. This is the parable of the prodigal son, the parable of the lost son, or, as it is sometimes called, the parable of the merciful father. Alongside the parables which Luke takes over from Mark and Matthew there is a whole series of parables which occur only in the Gospel of Luke: the parable of the rich farmer (Luke 12.13–21), the parable of the lost drachma (Luke 15.8–10), the parable of the crafty steward (Luke 16.1–8), the parable of the rich man and the poor Lazarus (Luke 16.19–31), and the parable of the godless judge and the widow (Luke 18.1–8). In these so-called special parables Luke often uses a typical Greek style, above all making use of soliloquy. In Greek literature the inner monologue has the function of disclosing a person's character, worries or concerns. We find this literary means above all in the romance literature of antiquity and in Greek and Latin comedies, for example in Menander, Plautus and Terence. However, the tragedies of Aeschylus, Sophocles and Euripides also make use of monologue. In the ancient love story the inner monologue serves to deepen the reader's involvement. Readers slip into the role of the characters in the romance. In the romance *Callirhoe* Artaxtares says to himself: 'Examine what is possible for you, my soul. Come to yourself. You have no other adviser.' This is very reminiscent of the soliloquy of the rich farmer with his soul. In comedy the monologues are a dialogue with the audience. The audience is drawn into what is happening. The monologue creates a secret and inner bond between the audience and the character; here the audience is as it were let into the actor's confidence.

The inner monologue begins with an introduction. Often enough it's the question, 'What shall I do?' Then follows a stocktaking. The various possibilities are discussed. And lastly a solution to the problem is presented. The inner monologue is meant to move readers to new action, to repentance, so that they take the right course. However, the question 'What shall we do?' is not limited in Luke to the inner monologue. It is also put by the tax collectors and soldiers to John the Baptist (Luke 3.10, 12, 13). It is the reaction of the inhabitants of Jerusalem to Peter's sermon at Pentecost (Acts 2.38). It is the basic question of authentic philosophy. Thus the Stoic philosopher Epictetus asks, 'What shall we do? That is the question of an honest disciple of philosophy who feels the birth pangs of the truth.' Luke doesn't invent his parables. Rather, he takes up the parables of Jesus and gives them literary form in such a way that the Greeks feel that they are being addressed. He wants to present Jesus to his Greek leaders as a poet who introduces them to the mystery of the human soul, who reveals to them secret thoughts and teaches them the true philosophy, the wisdom of God that leads to true life.

Moreover in the special parables we recognize Luke's tendency to give examples from the world of women as well as from the world of men. So alongside the parable of the lost sheep (Luke 15.3–7), which comes from the world of male shepherds, he creates the parable of the lost drachma, in which a woman is the main character (Luke 15.8–10). Alongside the crafty steward (Luke 16.1–8) he puts the courageous widow who is not afraid of the godless judge (Luke 18.1–18). Jesus compares the kingdom of heaven both to the mustardseed which a man puts in the earth and to the leaven which a woman mixes with a measure of flour (Luke 13.18–21). Luke can describe the mystery of divine activity and the mystery of human beings only by describing the way in which men and women act and think. For Luke, to talk properly about God means to combine *anima* and *animas*, to see the masculine and the feminine in God. And we can speak of people rightly only if we look at men and women with equal love and attempt to fathom the different ways in which each of them think.

The parable of the lost drachma

The brief parable of the lost drachma (Luke 15.8–10) follows the parable of the lost sheep. A woman is at the centre of it. It is interesting that Luke often depicts women as widows or as living alone. The woman is not defined by the man. She is herself. So in the case of this woman, too, the issue is not her relationship to her husband, but her selfhood, her independence. She has ten drachmae. Ten is the number of totality. Someone who has ten drachmae is whole and well. But the woman has lost a drachma. One is likewise the image of unity. When the woman has lost one drachma, she has lost her totality, her unity with herself and with God. She has lost her centre. And without this centre the nine other drachmae are useless to her. Everything falls apart. There are no longer any links. The woman knows what she has lost. She has lost herself. Gregory of Nyssa interprets the drachma as an image of Christ. Psychologically speaking, one could say that the drachma symbolizes the self. Those who have lost themselves may still seem to do a lot, but they lack a centre, power, clarity.

Now the woman lights a lamp. For Gregory that is the mind. She needs the light of the mind to illuminate the darkness of the unconscious and in it to seek the totality she has lost. Here Luke certainly also seems to be thinking of the light of faith. Only through faith is the mind really illuminated. We need the light of God to seek the drachma within us. The woman sweeps out the whole house. She sweeps away the dirt which has been lying on the floor of her house. Gregory interprets this dirt as an image of our inattentiveness. If we engage in many activities without being sufficiently attentive, our house gets dirty. We are no longer masters in the house. There is a layer of dust on the floor of our soul. So we must sweep vigorously in order to regain the original splendour of our soul. And the woman seeks tirelessly. The Greek word *epimelos* means 'anxiously, carefully, closely, zealously'. The woman looks round carefully and searches anxiously. She is concerned to find her drachma again. Human beings aren't just in search of God but also in search of themselves, their true being. They've lost themselves. That's their disaster: alienation from themselves, a loss of self.

The woman finds her drachma. She finds herself. Now she summons her friends and neighbours: 'Rejoice with me; I have found the drachma that I had lost' (Luke 15.9). Those who find themselves also find a new relationship to their fellow men and women. The woman summons only women. She wants to celebrate with them the feast of her becoming a self. She has found the lost drachma. She has found God as the foundation of her humanity. And she has found herself. According to Jung, we cannot find the self without discovering the image of God in our soul. The self is not the result of our life history, but the model that God has made of us. In the finding of the drachma Luke sees the sinner who repents. The sinner has lost himself. He is no longer himself. To repent means to think differently, to see behind things. Repentance is the way by which we discover our true self. We must get beyond the superficial and open ourselves up, in order to find the drachma in the depth of our soul. Then, Jesus tells us, God's angels will rejoice over us. Jesus has come to remind us of our divine nucleus. He has called on us to repent so that we find God in ourselves and our true self in God. Jesus is the one who calls us to the way of becoming selves. The goal of this way is the joy of being human. However, we are whole persons only when we have found God, when we have rediscovered the divine nucleus in us. Sin consists in failing ourselves and losing ourselves, in missing out on life. According to Luke, Jesus is the one who invites people to be truly human again, to find their centre – and in this centre to find God as the true ground of their being.

A parable always has different levels. It leaves readers the freedom to project their own experiences and longings on to it. The woman with the drachma can be an image of the human soul that has lost its centre and is now in search of its true self. But she can also be an image of God, who seeks the lost and turns everything upside down in doing so. If we interpret the parables in this way, then God is being described with the image of a woman. Nowhere in the Old Testament is God compared with a woman rummaging through the house. It is precisely when we've got the house of our life in good order that God acts like a woman who turns everything upside down in search of a drachma. We've sorted things out well at the centre of our life but by an excessive concern for externals we've lost the drachma. So God causes a crisis to make us look for the drachma, our true selves.

But we can also interpret this parable in terms of Jesus. In that case Jesus understands his own action as that of a wife and mother. In Jesus God sent his Son to kindle the light of faith in the world, to sweep out the room and tirelessly look for people. Jesus goes in particular to the sinners and tax collectors whom the Pharisees thought to be 'lost'. But the action of the woman also describes the activity of Jesus in the individual's soul. Jesus kindles a light in the human house so that we may recognize ourselves, so that we may see into the depths of our souls. Jesus sweeps out the room of the soul; by his word he drives out of it all the demons, all the patterns of life that prevent people from living. And he tirelessly seeks out the human self. For the great Greek philosopher Plato that was the aim of human life: to find the true self, to recognize the original soul. For Luke, Jesus is the divine wanderer who puts people in contact with their true selves, with the divine nucleus within them.

The parable of the lost son

The parable of the lost or prodigal son is probably the most beautiful parable that Luke tells us. It has been interpreted in countless ways. That shows that the text moves the reader. Telling a parable is more than proclaiming a theological truth. The parables don't seek to inform or prove; they want to compel us to adopt a position. Linguistic scholars speak of 'persuasive communication'. In telling a parable, Jesus brings something about in the hearer. We can't read the parable of the lost son as Luke tells it to us without becoming inwardly involved in a process of transformation. The younger and the older son confront us with the questions 'Where do I stand? Am I more the younger or the older son? Or am I both?' The motif of the two brothers in particular indicates the inner polarity of our souls. We have in us the younger son, who just wants to live it up, with no concern for law or moderation. And we have in us the conformist older brother, who works hard to observe all the commandments. We are to look at both sides and combine the two opposite poles in us. The parable doesn't raise any warning moralistic finger, so that we have to repent and do penance. Rather, Jesus tells the parable in such a way that we cannot avoid asking where we've gone astray, where we're feeding on cheap stuff, and whether we've lost ourselves. By reading the parable I am moved in my heart to make my way to the Father, where I am really at home.

There are many similar examples to the parable of the prodigal son in Greek literature. There we often find the motif of sons confessing to their fathers that they have squandered their possessions on prostitutes. The Roman comedy writer Plautus tells of a father who has lost his two sons. When he finds them again he holds a feast. Since Aristophanes the 'good youth and the bad youth' are a well-known pair in Greek comedy. These examples show that Luke must have had a rhetorical training. He knows Greek literature with its romances, comedies, tragedies and fables. Luke uses his rhetorical training to address the reader directly. He writes in such a way that he enters into a dialogue with the reader. And he engages not only with the Greek reader but also with us. Luke has found a language which touches everyone's hearts. No one can evade the message of this parable.

The son is tired of the conformist life at home. He asks for his share of his inheritance from his father now. He wants to live, straight away. That's the attitude of many young people today. They just want to live, extravagantly and as soon as possible. The younger son goes to a distant land. There is nothing reprehensible about that. It shows his boldness. But then he squanders his money 'in a dissolute life'. In the Greek that is said to be *zon asotos* = 'he lived without hope of salvation; he lived in an unhealthy, unbridled, blasphemous way'. Aristotle defines *asotos* as 'someone who is in a desperate state, profligate, beyond recovery'. The son sinks so low that he hires himself out to work in the fields, looking after the pigs. For Jewish readers that is a picture of utter depravity, of someone who has lost all self-respect and dignity. He has landed up among the pigs, but he doesn't even get the husks the pigs eat. When he has reached rock bottom, when everything has been taken out of his hands, when he is sitting on the rubbish heap of his existence, empty and a failure, he looks at himself and comes to himself. Having become completely alienated from himself and given himself into the hands of someone else, he gets back into contact with himself, and returns to himself. When he comes to himself he engages in a monologue which accurately reflects his inner situation: 'How many of my father's hired men have all the food they want and more, and here I am dying of hunger (*apollymai* = 'I am getting lost, perishing'). I will set out (*anastas* = 'arise, stand up') and go to my father and say, "Father, I have sinned against heaven and against you. I no longer deserve to be called your son; treat me as one of your hired men"' (Luke 15.17ff.). This monologue depicts the spiritual state of the son and gives the reader an insight into his psyche. The son is close to abandoning himself completely. But there is a voice in him which makes him repent. He doesn't want to lose himself. He wants to live.

He acts in accordance with what he has seen in his heart. He sets off for his father. His father has compassion on him and runs to meet him. Haste was inappropriate for the head of a household. But the father cares nothing for his position. His son is more important to him. So he hastens to him, falls on his neck and kisses him. He doesn't let the son say a word but commands the servants to bring the son's garments, to put a ring on his finger and shoes on his feet. In doing this, the father takes the son right back into the family again. And he holds a banquet: 'We should celebrate and rejoice. For my son was dead and is alive; he was lost and is found' (Luke 15.23ff.).

Jesus tells the parable of the lost son to the Pharisees and scribes, who are furious that he is eating with sinners (Luke 15.2). With the parable he not only tells us who God is and how someone can repent and rediscover his salvation, but also explains his own actions. Jesus eats with the sinners in order to make God's mercy visible and possible to experience here on earth. He has come down from heaven to proclaim the merciful God, who has compassion on those who have lost themselves, who are inwardly dead, who are alienated from themselves. By eating and drinking with sinners Jesus is acting on behalf of the Father: he makes the merciful God appear in concrete. As Luke understands it, what Jesus does in eating with sinners happens at every celebration of the eucharist. There God celebrates a feast with us in which together with Christ we can rejoice that we who were dead have come to life again, and that we who were lost have found ourselves again. Thus in the parable Jesus also depicts his own mission. He understands himself as the one who calls those who were inwardly dead back to life, who conjures up life in them. And he understands his action as seeking those who are lost, who have come to grief. With his parable Jesus wants to awaken the hope of life in people who have given up on themselves. For them, too, repentance is possible. There is no reason to give up. However far we may have gone astray, satisfying our hunger with cheap stuff, we can return to the house of the Father in which we may truly be at home, in which we may be what God has made us, sons and daughters of the heavenly Father.

But Jesus' invitation to sinners comes up against resistance. In the parable the older son appears and is furious at the joyful festivities. The Old Testament knows how angry the believer is when God has mercy on sinners. Thus Jonah reacts angrily to the mercy that God shows to Nineveh. And the psalmist speaks of the wrath of the pious at the success of the evil (Ps. 37.1). Each of the three characters in the parable of the lost son is characterized by his feelings: the younger son gets introspective, the father feels pity and the older brother becomes angry. The older son stands not only for the Pharisees, who take great care to fulfil God's commandments but in so doing often do their duty in a joyless way, without discovering the riches of life which God offers them. All readers will rediscover themselves in the older son. We often live out the ideal of fulfilling all God's commandments and doing only his will. But our fury at others who don't observe the commandments shows that our conformity doesn't spring from pure motives: it doesn't make us happy. Often enough anxiety about life underlies it. If the younger son lives out our shadow side (our suppressed liveliness), we become angry.

The unconscious motives that may have made the older son stay at home, be good and conform, become evident in his words to his father: 'All these years I have slaved for you and have never once disobeyed any orders of yours, yet you never offered me so much as a kid for me to celebrate with my friends. But for this son of yours, when he comes back after swallowing up your property – he and his loose women – you kill the calf we had been fattening' (Luke 15.29f.). The son has not been unselfishly fulfilling his father's will; he wanted to earn recognition by doing so. He secretly expected that his father would single him out specially because he remained at home, that he would prefer him to the younger son. And behind the façade of good behaviour we can detect suppressed sexual fantasies. For his accusation that the younger brother has been swallowing up his property with loose women doesn't fit the story. It's a figment of his imagination. In the older brother Luke describes our shadow sides, which are often enough hidden behind a pious façade.

The father also turns lovingly to the older son: 'My son, you are with me always and all that I have is yours. But it was only right that we should celebrate and rejoice, because your brother here was dead and has come to life; he was lost and is found' (Luke 15.31f.). This is a very tender remark to make to the older son. And yet the father points out that 'this son of yours' is also his brother. If the brother who had gone astray has been found again and if the one who was dead is alive again, there is reason enough to have a happy feast.

We cannot read this parable without coming into contact with our own wishes and needs, our emotions and longings. Both brothers discover what is hidden in our soul. And both sons point to the merciful Father. We can turn to him whether we are the younger or the older son, the one who goes astray or the one who behaves, the reckless one or the conformist one. Both were dead in their own way and both had got lost, one in a life of debauchery, the other in anxious rectitude. The merciful father invites us to life, to a joyful feast, to find life in ourselves and to enjoy it.

The parable of the crafty steward

I now want to look briefly at another parable special to Luke: the parable of the crafty steward (Luke 16.1–8). This parable can still provoke the reader today. When I attempt to interpret the parable in a group there are always protests. Surely Jesus can't approve of deception! With this parable we detect the psychological skill with which Jesus addresses the reader. By provoking his hearers, Jesus lures them from the safe position of their piety. At the precise point where a parable offends us, we are challenged to put our view of God and human beings in question and to correct it.

With his parable about the unjust steward who tricks his master, Jesus surely provoked a sense of *Schadenfreude* among his audience, which is to be sought more among the poor. But that isn't the issue. The issue is how we deal with our guilt. Whether we want to or not, we are blamed or accused. We've no chance of getting out of it. The question is how we react to this, whether we're ashamed of it all our lives and go around in penitential garments, as the steward thinks of doing in his monologue. In that case we keep disparaging ourselves and look for attention. The other possible way of reacting to guilt would be to work hard, to grit our teeth, so that from now on we did everything right and scrupulously obeyed all the commandments. But neither way gets anywhere. In his monologue the steward finds a third way, which Jesus approves of. Instead of working off our guilt before God or becoming utterly ashamed, we are to use this guilt as an opportunity to enter into relations with others. The steward does the only thing possible. He summons the debtors and reduces their debt. By doing this he hopes that people will receive him into their houses. He deals creatively with his guilt. He's imaginative about the way in which he can make the best of it. Jesus praises the craftiness of the dishonest steward: 'The children of this world are wiser in dealing with their like than the children of light' (Luke 16.8). The expression 'children of light' recalls the Essenes, who were very pious, but mercilessly expelled all those who transgressed their norms. Things are not to be like that in the Christian community. Christians are not to exclude one another but to welcome people into their houses when they have incurred guilt. Jesus speaks of guilt here in a very matter-of-fact way. In the church we haven't yet caught up with his open and clear language. Particularly when we are talking about guilt we are in danger of disparaging and devaluing people. We inculcate feelings of guilt in them so that they will show repentance. We can learn from Jesus how to deal with guilt and guilt feelings in a different way. Jesus wants to show us a way of dealing with our guilt without losing our self-respect.

6

Jesus – A Model for Prayer

More than any other evangelist, Luke has described Jesus as someone who prayed. Jesus is the great man of prayer. He prays at the most important events of his life. He prays before decisions. Time and again Jesus withdraws to lonely places in order to pray to his Father. When Luke writes about Jesus as someone who prays, he always has the believing Christian in view. For him prayer is above all a way of surmounting the tribulations in life. Just as Jesus surmounts his passion with prayer, so Christians are to persevere in prayer to God, in order to attain glory through all their tribulations. Prayer is a way of practising Jesus' attitude and being permeated by his spirit.

Jesus shows what could also happen for us in prayer. Jesus prays at his baptism, and heaven opens above him (Luke 3.21). That's a splendid image of the effect of prayer. When we pray, heaven opens above us. In prayer the Holy Spirit descends on us. And we experience in prayer that we are unconditionally loved by God. In prayer we recognize who we really are. When Jesus healed the lepers and people streamed in from all sides, he withdrew 'to a lonely place to pray' (Luke 5.16). Prayer is a protected area to which we may withdraw in order to be safe from the tumult of the world and the expectations of others. Before Jesus chose twelve apostles from his disciples, he spent the whole night on the mountain in prayer to God (Luke 6.12). Prayer enables us to make good decisions. Before Peter's confession of Jesus' messiahship, Jesus prays in solitude (Luke 9.18). Evidently he is preparing himself by prayer to initiate the disciples into the mystery of his suffering and their way of discipleship of the cross.

Only Luke tells us how Jesus prayed at his transfiguration: 'As he was praying, the aspect of his face was changed and his clothing became sparkling white' (Luke 9.29). In prayer we come in contact with our true being. All superficiality falls away. The masks behind which we hide shatter. Transfiguration means that our authentic, original beauty shines through. God's radiance which is in us shines from our face. We recognize that we are the glory of God. When Jesus is transfigured, Moses and Elijah appear. Moses is the lawgiver and the liberator. When we pray, our life gets sorted out, and we experience true freedom in God. What people think about us is no longer so important. Elijah is the prophet. In prayer we discover our prophetic mission. We have an inkling that we can express something with our lives that can only become visible in this world through us. In prayer – we are told by the story of the transfiguration of Jesus – we come into contact with our true selves, and God's glory shines out in us. However, we can't hang on to this experience of prayer. It vanishes again. A cloud again obscures our vision and we have to go back alone with the memory of this experience of light into the often misty valley of our everyday life.

Luke depicts the high point of Jesus' prayer in the passion. On the Mount of Olives Jesus prays and struggles with the will of God. An angel appears to him from heaven and strengthens him. Prayer isn't always just a peaceful experience. It can also be a painful struggle for the will of God. But God sends his angel to those who pray, to give them new strength. However, the angel doesn't preserve Jesus from fear. Jesus becomes afraid of death. He sweats for fear. But at that very moment he prays all the more urgently (Luke 22.44). Luke relates this scene of prayer on the Mount of Olives against the background of the difficulty that many people, today as then, have with prayer. In prayer we often experience darkness. Prayer is useless. It doesn't achieve anything. God hides behind a thick wall. He seems to be silent. Because we can't get through to God, we often feel like the disciples. We go to sleep. Our prayer goes to sleep. And Jesus has to shake us awake: 'Get up and pray, so as not to be put to the test' (Luke 22.46). We find ourselves in the same tribulation as Jesus, in solitude, anxiety, abandonment, in distress and sorrow. For us prayer is the way of resisting temptations, as Jesus did, and of holding fast to God even in the greatest tribulation.

His prayer on the Mount of Olives evidently gives Jesus the strength to endure the way of the passion. It gives him the certainty that even in death he cannot fall out of God's good hands. Jesus' prayer culminates in his prayer on the cross. Hanging on the cross, Jesus prays not only for himself but also for his murderers: 'Father, forgive them, for they know not what they do' (Luke 23.34). And Jesus dies with a prayer on his lips. It's a verse from Psalm 31, the Jewish evening prayer. Like a pious Jew, at the end of his life Jesus prays, 'Father, into your hands I commit my spirit' (Luke 23.46). But Jesus adds his intimate form of address, 'Abba', to the words of the psalm. Even on the cross he tenderly addresses God as his Father. He commits his spirit to the loving hands of his Father. In death he returns to the Father. The prayer transfigures his dying. Despite all the cruelty, Jesus persists in prayer and so remains in contact with God in his greatest distress. Indeed his relationship with God frees him from the power of men. Even his murderers cannot triumph over him. Prayer lifts him into another world, which the cries of his executioners cannot penetrate. Thus prayer accompanies Jesus from the beginning of his activity to his end on the cross. It shows where Jesus has found his true support. And it reveals that in the power of prayer Jesus could go his way even through the greatest tribulation of death, because beyond all the suffering heaven stood open, and he knew that he was one with the Father.

Jesus' teaching about prayer

If the prayer of Jesus has such a healing and liberating effect, no wonder that the disciples ask him, 'Lord, teach us to pray' (Luke 11.1). In Luke's Gospel, Jesus shows the disciples not only what they should pray but above all how and with what attitude they should pray. Jesus tells the disciples what Christians are to pray in the words of the Our Father. Many exegetes think that Luke has preserved the original version of the Our Father. Luke always has great respect for the original resonance of the words of Jesus: 'Father, hallowed be your name, your kingdom come, give us the bread we need for every day, and forgive us our sins, for we also forgive those who have sinned against us, and lead us not into temptation.' Jesus always addressed God as Father. In the prayer that he teaches us he lets us share in his relationship to the Father. The name is the reality of God. It is to be hallowed. It is to become visible in our world and be acknowledged by all. The kingdom is God's glory. It is to become established in the world. But it is also in us. When God's image shines out in the depth of our hearts, God's kingdom has come to us. The bread for which we are to pray isn't just material bread, but at the same time the bread of friendship and fellowship. And it is the heavenly, divine bread. It is the living bread of the eucharist. In the petition for forgiveness Luke replaces the word 'debts' with the word 'sins'. For the Greek word 'debt' doesn't relate to the violation of divine commandments. Sins (*hamartiai*) are transgressions, missed opportunities, failed goals, omissions. The last petition doesn't mean that we remain preserved from temptations but that God protects us in them. The Aramaic Lord's Prayer probably understood this petition to mean 'Grant that we do not enter into temptation'. Even the Greeks don't think that God himself leads people into temptation. But they aren't spared temptations. God is to give us the power not to succumb to temptations when they arise. With his version of the Lord's Prayer Luke is addressing the newly converted. They recite the prayer in remembrance of the words of Jesus. It becomes the most important feature of their devotions. In its words they come into contact with the spirit of Jesus, with his personal experiences of prayer. Thus the Didache, which was composed at the end of the first century, prescribes that every Christian should pray the Lord's Prayer three times a day. And it was prayed before communion at every eucharist. Before we receive the body of Christ we become one with his spirit, which is expressed most clearly in the Our Father.

Luke sheds light on how we should pray, and with what attitude, by two parables which he puts after the Our Father. The parable of the friend's request (Luke 11.5–8) has in view a Palestinian village in which there are no shops. Every house provides its own food. A visitor arrives in the middle of the night and there is nothing to offer him. That's painful, for hospitality is the greatest good in the East and in Greece. So the householder goes to his friend and knocks on the door. He knows the difficulties he is causing his friend. The friend has to get up and open the door, which is secured with a beam. The noise he makes in removing the beam will wake up the children. But hospitality is a sacred duty. So he will get up and give his friend all he needs. With this parable Jesus wants to tell us that God is our friend. And Luke interprets this parable like a Greek philosopher: we Christians are God's friends. Praying is speaking to God as to a friend. We may make requests of God as shamelessly as of a friend. God will not turn us away. For the friendship between God and us is far firmer than that between human beings.

Only Luke tells us the parable of the friend's request. As a Greek, Luke loves the word 'friend'. Whereas Mark and Matthew use the word 'friend' only once, in Luke we find it eighteen times. For Greeks, friendship was a great good. The Greeks were regarded as the classical example of friendship. Socrates and Plato wrote about friendship. Friendship is possible only between good people. In the Gospel of Luke Jesus calls his disciples friends (Luke 12.4). Luke depicts the community in Jerusalem as a Hellenistic group of friends. So it's natural for him to apply the image of the friend to our relationship with God. The mystery of friendship is revealed only when we experience God in prayer as our friend, who gives us something that we need for life and love.

The second parable explains what it means to have God as Father. Every father knows what is good for his children. The human heart is thoroughly good. The father cares for his children. He will not give them a stone instead of bread, or a serpent instead of a fish, or a scorpion instead of an egg. Here Jesus is speaking to people's sense of honesty. Readers are moved by these examples which are attributed to an earthly father. God is our good Father. He knows what is good for us. He will not disappoint us and will not give us anything that could harm us. He gives us nourishment. Augustine interprets the three gifts symbolically. The bread means love, the fish faith and the egg hope. A good father doesn't give his son the stone of harshness and rejection instead of love. He believes in his son and doesn't harm him like a serpent. And he gives him hope, and will not poison him with his bitterness or guilt feelings like a scorpion. God is the good Father who gives us the best gift that he has to give, the Holy Spirit. In the Holy Spirit God gives us himself. Then he is near to us. The Holy Spirit heals the wounds inflicted by our father when after all he does give us the stone, the serpent or the scorpion, and in so doing hurts us deeply. For Luke, prayer is the place where we may experience the healing of the wounds caused by our fathers and mothers.

The widow and the godless judge

Luke continues his instruction on prayer in chapter 18 of his Gospel. There as a counterpart he introduces a parable with a woman at the centre. This accords with his tendency to say something on all the important things from the side of both men and women. When Luke is talking about prayer, too, he can speak appropriately only if he offers examples from both the world of the man and the world of the woman. Whereas in chapter 11 Luke understands his teaching on prayer as the fulfilment of the love of God, in chapter 18 he speaks of prayer in the oppressive situation before the coming of the Son of man. The woman, the widow who is oppressed by an enemy (Luke 18.1–8), stands for the threatened Christian community which turns to the state authorities in vain. For the judge does not fear God and pays heed to no one. But the widow can also be understood as a type of the individual. Then she represents the personal situation of those oppressed by enemies, who are hurt by others and can't defend themselves against them. The woman who has lost her husband is as it were an image of the person with a thin skin, exposed without protection to the emotional pressures of the environment. These are unbounded. All the negative elements of their environment invade such people. The woman has always also been an image of the soul, our inner sphere, the intimations of our divine dignity. The enemies stand for the patterns of life which hinder us from living, for our weaknesses which cause us trouble, and for the wounds which have damaged our life. The judge who cares about neither God nor man symbolizes the superego, the inner authority which wants to do us down, which has no interest in our well-being. It's concerned only with norms and principles. The soul is to be still and content with what it finds.

The apparently powerless woman fights for herself. She keeps going to the judge and demanding of him, 'I want justice from you against my enemy!' (Luke 18.3). The judge engages in a monologue, again in the typical style of Greek comedies. 'Even though I have neither fear of God nor respect for any human person, I must give this widow her just rights since she keeps pestering me, or she will come and slap me in the face' (Luke 18.5). The Greek word used here literally means 'give a black eye'. The listener may chuckle, because this powerful judge is afraid of the weak widow who could give him a black eye. But with this particular remark by the judge, Luke convinces the reader to trust the means of prayer, which is apparently so weak. In prayer men and women get justice. They have a right to life, a right to help, a right to dignity. In prayer we may experience that people have no power over us. Just as the murderers could not triumph over Jesus, who prayed on the cross, so those who oppress us have no power over us. If we take the widow as an image of the soul, that means that in prayer we experience that the soul has more rights than the voices of the superego which wants to do us down. The soul flourishes in prayer. It takes wing. In prayer we come into contact with our true self, with the original image of God in us. The world cannot disturb or even destroy the image of God in our soul.

The Pharisee and the tax collector

Luke knows the danger that our ideals in the spiritual life may be too high. He speaks of constant prayer. But such an ideal image of praying always also has a shadow side. We are then in danger of putting ourselves above others with our prayer. We feel that we're better than the others. Luke guards against this danger of forming one-sided ideals by presenting us with the opposite pole, in the parable of the Pharisee and the tax collector (Luke 18.9–14). The Pharisee's prayer is a pious reflection of himself. He is completely self-centred. In this parable Luke shows us two ways of praying: the prayer of the self-righteous Pharisee and the prayer of the humble tax collector. Even from the outside the prayers of the Pharisee and the tax collector are different. Whereas the prayer of the Pharisee is long, the prayer of the tax collector is striking for its brevity. By contrast, the Pharisee's preparation for his prayer is short. He simply stands up and begins to pray. But the tax collector remains at the back, dares not look up and beats his breast. He expresses his prayer above all through his body. The Pharisee is completely self-centred in his prayer. He uses God to put himself in the right light. He isn't concerned with God but with his own self-righteousness. The Greek words are literally, 'He prayed to himself.' Certainly the Pharisee says, 'God, I thank you that I am not like everyone else' (Luke 18.11). But really he remains by himself in prayer. He doesn't look up to God but only at himself. Many pious people think that they're praying to God. But they aren't. They're praying to themselves. They worship themselves. They misuse prayer to boost themselves, to put themselves in the right light before God and their fellow human beings. By contrast, the tax collector senses how remote he is from God. He recognizes before God who he really is. So he beats his breast and prays, 'God be merciful to me a sinner' (Luke 18.13). Now Jesus gives his commentary on these two ways of praying. The tax collector goes home from his prayer justified. He has recognized his own truth before God and has shown due repentance. The Pharisee has used God only for his own ends. Only the prayer in which we offer ourselves unsparingly to God will direct us to God and justify us.

In his teaching about prayer Luke doesn't just hand on Jesus' sayings about prayer. Rather, the person of the author himself makes an appearance. Luke isn't only a literary man open to the world and aware of problems, with his finger on the pulse of time. He is also a pious man. For him prayer is the place in which he encounters God and grows into the spirit of Jesus. Prayer for him is also the experience of the resurrection. Luke has described that for us in the Acts of the Apostles. In that book Luke speaks 25 times of prayer. The earliest church is a praying community. When the community prayed, the place shook, there was movement, and all 'were filled with the Holy Spirit' (Acts 4.31). When Peter was in prison, the community prayed 'urgently for him to God' (Acts 12.5). God sends his angel to Peter in prison. Peter's chains drop off, and the doors open. In prayer we may experience God's protection and loving care in the midst of the tribulations of our life. In prayer we share in the spirit of Jesus. In prayer we learn, like Jesus, to turn to the Father. In prayer God is near to us as Father and friend. In prayer we experience a right to live. Only those who pray understand what Jesus wanted to communicate to us with his message and his life. As we pray, we grow into the spirit of Jesus. As we pray, we experience redemption. For in prayer the powers of this world are robbed of their power, and guilt feelings lose their strength. The tombs open, and with Christ we rise to the true life, to life in God.

7

Jesus as the Divine Traveller

What marks out Luke's Gospel from Mark's, on which it is based, is the so-called travel account, which extends from Luke 9.51 to Luke 19.27. Luke depicts Jesus here as travelling to Jerusalem, the city of fulfilment, the city to which all God's promises apply. But for Jesus the way to Jerusalem is also the way to suffering, to death and to resurrection. In his travel account Luke depicts the way of Jesus as the model for our way. Jesus is the guide to life. He goes before us. Our task is to follow him. Then our way will also lead us to true life.

Not only in this travel account but throughout the Gospel Luke depicts Jesus as the divine traveller. He comes down from heaven to travel with us human beings and time and again to be our guest. That's a typically Greek motif. The Greek myths tell of gods who appear in human form and appear to people to test their character and to give them gifts. Luke takes up this motif but changes it. Jesus doesn't test people but instructs them and shows them God's loving care. In Jesus, God himself visits people. The motif of God's visit already rings out twice in Zechariah's song of praise: 'He has visited and redeemed his people' (Luke 1.68), and 'By the merciful love of our God the radiance from on high will visit us' (Luke 1.78). At the resurrection of the young man of Nain the people confesses, 'A great prophet has risen up among us; God has visited his people' (Luke 7.16). The Greek word *episkeptomai* = 'visit' really means 'see, oversee, inspect, consider'. So the Greeks imagine that God comes to earth in Jesus to take a closer look at men and women and give them a broader horizon. Jesus has come to us from heaven to remind us of our divine nucleus. That is a motif from Platonic philosophy. Every human being is an idea of God. But we have obscured and distorted this idea. Jesus comes to us from God; he looks at us so that we again become capable of seeing ourselves in the right light, discovering the divine nucleus in ourselves and thus coming into contact with our true being.

The second motif connected with the image of the divine traveller is that of staying with people. Jesus keeps staying with people to have a meal with them. As a divine guest he brings with him tokens of hospitality: salvation and peace, grace (*charis*) and joy. At the meal Jesus doesn't just speak of God's goodness and loving-kindness but communicates them by being there, by eating and drinking, by the fellowship which links him with those who are celebrating. No evangelist has reported Jesus at so many meals as Luke has. That's a typically Greek motif. Xenophon and Plato develop their philosophy at banquets, at symposia. There is a rich symposium literature in Greek philosophy. Luke has taken up this motif. Jesus teaches people above all at meals. At the meal he shows God's gracious care for sinners, as he does at the meal with the tax collector Levi and his friends (Luke 5.27–32) and at the meal with a Pharisee, into which the woman who is a sinner forces her way in order to anoint Jesus' feet. Jesus explicitly announces God's forgiveness to her (Luke 7.48). He relates the heart of the Gospel, the parable of the prodigal son, at a meal (Luke 14 and 15). And he tells it in order to explain why he eats with sinners (Luke 15.1–2). Luke portrays Jesus' last meal with his disciples as a symposium. Jesus talks with the disciples about the essentials of faith and discipleship. And he also appears to the disciples at a meal after the resurrection. Especially in the marvellous story of the disciples on the road to Emmaus, Jesus is the traveller who goes with the disciples and has a meal with them. The Risen Christ also goes with us, often enough unrecognized. But when we break bread with one another he is present among us. Then the divine guest is with us to give us his love and to remind us that we are God's sons and daughters, that we have a divine dignity and a divine nucleus.

Luke loves the preposition *syn* = 'with'. We are with Jesus on the way; he takes us with him on the way of transformation. Jesus wants to mould us in his image. Luke shows that above all in the Acts of the Apostles. The motif of travelling shapes the activity of Jesus' disciples. The apostles travel through the Roman empire to hand on the message of Jesus. Filled with the power and the spirit of Jesus, they bring God's salvation to people. Whereas Jesus travels from Galilee to Jerusalem to fulfil his fate and thus God's promise there, the disciples travel from Jerusalem to Rome, the capital of the Roman empire. The centre of the world is brightened by Jesus' good news. The story of Jesus

reaches fulfilment only when the whole world is permeated with Jesus' spirit. People's reactions to Jesus' disciples
is like their reaction to Jesus. They have the impression
that God himself is visiting people in the disciples. When
Paul heals a paralysed man in Lystra, the people there
believe that the gods have come down to them in human
form (Acts 14.11f.). And when Paul brushes off the snake
that has bitten him without suffering any harm, the
onlookers think that 'he is a god' (Acts 28.6).

Luke begins the great travel account in which he depicts
Jesus' journey to Jerusalem with the words: 'Now it happened that as the time drew near for him to be taken up, he
resolutely turned his face towards Jerusalem and sent messengers ahead of him' (Luke 9.51). The word 'taken up',
which is typical of Luke, doesn't just mean the ascension
but the whole complex of death, resurrection and welcome
into heaven. In this being taken up Jesus' way reaches its
destination. He has come down from heaven. And now he
is taken up again into heaven. But the way to this destination leads through suffering and death. That also holds
for us, who with (*syn*) Jesus attain the kingdom of God
through many tribulations (Acts 14.22). Jesus is our guide in
life. As our leader he opens up for us the way to true life.
Thus by the motif of travelling Luke explains how he
understands redemption through Jesus. He avoids terms
like atonement and sacrifice, since they are incomprehensible to Greeks. And we also find such notions difficult
today. But we can easily understand that Jesus goes before
us and opens up for us the way to life. People have always
understood their life as a way. In the spiritual traditions we
know the various spiritual ways which lead us to God. As

human beings we are always on the way. We can't stand still. We change as we travel. Jesus understands his life as perpetual travel: 'I must travel today, and tomorrow, and the next day' (Luke 13.33). The destination of his travels is Jerusalem, 'Since it would not be right for a prophet to die outside Jerusalem' (Luke 13.33). By describing Jesus' way to Jerusalem, the place of his suffering, Luke wants to encourage us to tread confidently and boldly through all the tribulations which we encounter on our way. For the glory of God awaits us too. We too will be taken up in death into the kingdom of God, into heaven. The death and resurrection of Jesus are to rid us of the fear of the dangers and crises in our lives, of the failure and collapse of our plans. All these are only the tribulations through which we enter into God's glory in fellowship with Jesus.

On the way Jesus is accompanied not only by men but equally by women. Only Luke explicitly mentions women as companions of Jesus: 'With him went the Twelve, as well as certain women who had been cured of evil spirits and ailments: Mary surnamed the Magdalene, from whom seven demons had gone out, Joanna the wife of Herod's steward Chuza, Susanna, and many others who had provided for them out of their own resources' (Luke 8.1–3). The women accompany Jesus until his death on the cross. And they are the first to hasten to the tomb of Jesus, in which they meet two angels who announce the resurrection of Jesus to them: 'He is not here, he is risen. Remember what he told you when he was still in Galilee' (Luke 24.6). This 'you' shows that in Galilee Jesus spoke not only to the male disciples but always also to the women. They too are disciples of Jesus. That also applies to the Christian community. For Luke, men and women are on an equal footing as disciples of Jesus. Indeed, the women are sometimes the first to understand the meaning of the words of Jesus, whereas often enough the men regard what the women experience and talk about as gossip (Luke 24.11).

Luke describes the way of the Christian as discipleship. It is our task to follow Jesus. That becomes clear at the beginning of the great travel account. Jesus has been rejected by the Samaritans. He is the homeless one, who wanders around in this world without finding acceptance. This homelessness is an essential feature of our being Christians. Luke describes it in a narrative: 'As they travelled along, they met a man on the road who said to him, "I will follow you wherever you go." Jesus answered, "Foxes have holes and the birds of the air have nests, but the Son of man has nowhere to lay his head." Another to whom he said, "Follow me," replied, "Let me go and bury my father first." But he answered, "Leave the dead to bury their dead; your duty is to go and spread the news of the kingdom of God." Another said, "I will follow you, Lord, but first let me go and say goodbye to my people at home." Jesus said to him, "Once the hand is laid on the plough, no one who looks back is fit for the kingdom of God"' (Luke 9.57–62). Here are three pictures of the discipleship which Luke is presenting to us. To follow Jesus therefore means to know that here we have no abiding stay. Neither our family nor our house offers a nest into which we can creep. We human beings have a divine nucleus. That drives us further along our way until we find our home in God. Jesus answers the one who wants to follow him with a proverb which was also known to the Greeks. Whereas the animals all have their homes, the human being doesn't. The only house in which he can truly be at home is God, to whom he belongs in all his being.

The second image of discipleship culminates in Jesus' provocative remark, 'Leave the dead to bury their dead.' In Israel it was a sacred duty to bury one's dead father. Jesus certainly doesn't want to call on people to evade this duty. His remark is meant metaphorically. Some people don't find their own way, the way that God has intended for them, because they are still too dependent on their fathers. They haven't yet buried their fathers. They are still too influenced by them. Taking the way of discipleship means freeing oneself from all family ties. The kingdom of God is more important than one's relationship with one's father. If God rules in the human heart, then the expectations of one's earthly father no longer need to be fulfilled. The way of Jesus leads to freedom, and he shows us what really matters. Burying one's father, wearing oneself out in arguments, is death by comparison with the life that Jesus opens up to us through his word and example.

Whereas the first two images of discipleship also appear in a shorter form in Matthew's Gospel (Matt. 8.18–22), the third image has been handed down only by Luke. With this image he has in view not only the disciples at the time of Jesus but also us Christians. Many people want to take the way that they have recognized in their hearts as theirs. They want to follow the voice of Jesus in their inner life. But first they want to bid farewell to their family. They want to explain their way to everyone. And perhaps they want everyone to approve of it. But Jesus again uses a radical proverb to call on them to follow their inner calling without looking to the right or the left, without safeguarding themselves and getting the approval of friends and relations. When it dawns on me in my heart who Jesus is and where he wants to lead me, I must follow him without looking back. Those who look back and want to check whether the furrow they have drawn in the field of their soul is straight are the ones who are incapable of really cultivating the field. Nothing will grow in it. The kingdom of God opens up our view forwards. What Jesus means by this saying is that God is such a radical reality that everything else pales beside it. God drives us on our way. He opens up the future to us. We are to bury the past with its hurts, its nostalgia, in order to be free for the moment, free for what God wants of us at any moment.

For Jesus, discipleship is discipleship of the cross. Twice in the Gospel of Luke Jesus invites the disciples to bear his cross: 'No one who does not carry his cross and come after me can be my disciple' (Luke 14.27). And, 'If anyone wants to be my disciple, let him renounce himself and take up his cross every day and follow me' (Luke 9.23). The first saying shows how serious discipleship is. Those who follow Jesus must reckon that their way will also lead to the cross, to persecution, to hostility, and finally to death. The second saying interprets discipleship of the cross as a spiritual way. Here Luke adds the words 'every day'. Here the cross has become the image of daily tribulations and conflicts. Every day something thwarts us. Every day people disappoint and hurt us. If we understand these daily challenges as the cross, we will not break on them, but for us the cross will lead to a deeper fellowship with Christ. The cross breaks apart our image of ourselves. We often in fact go through everyday life with an illusory ideal picture of ourselves. We think that we shall do God's will, we shall do our duty. If someone then criticizes us and treats us unfairly, if we're hurt and insulted, then we are often enough offended and complain about our situation. Jesus wants to invite us to break out of these daily tribulations and leave them to God. For me that means denying myself. This remark about denying oneself has often enough been understood wrongly, as if we were completely to abandon ourselves, devalue ourselves or evade ourselves. The Greek word *arneisthai* means 'say no, offer resistance, become detached'. By the experiences of the cross in my life I am to deny my ego, which inflates itself and has the illusion that everyone is at its service, in order to discover my real self. I am to become detached from the ego which wants to snatch everything for itself so that under this ego I can recognize the nucleus of my own person. This saying of Jesus isn't an invitation to me to make life particularly difficult for myself and load myself with burdens; it's an invitation to break out from life and its everyday tribulations and seek God. Then life will lead me to God. Then the cross will become the key to life. It will open the door for me to the depths of my soul, to my own depths. In these depths I will experience who I really am, beyond success and feeling good, beyond recognition and acknowledgement, beyond criticism and insults.

8

The Passion Narrative

Like Mark and Matthew, Luke relates the passion of Jesus, his way through the cross to resurrection. But Luke interprets the passion of Jesus in his own fashion. First, he describes the way of Jesus through suffering to death on the cross and resurrection in such a manner that we can recognize our way in it. By his narrative of the passion, Luke wants to invite us to follow our own way of the cross. A look at Jesus' way will encourage us not to evade the tribulations which meet us on our way, but to endure them. Just as Jesus makes his way through the cross to the resurrection, so too we are 'to enter the kingdom of God through many tribulations' (Acts 14.22). Luke sees the passion of Jesus in his humanity. Jesus is the truly just man, who shows how we are to go our way rightly, how in the midst of suffering we can hold on to our loving-kindness (the Greek ideal of *philanthropia*).

The second motif which guides Luke in his story of the passion is the motif of redemption. Luke wants to demonstrate how this Jesus has redeemed us, saved us, healed us through his death and resurrection. In doing this he dispenses with Jewish concepts like atonement and sacrifice, which the Greeks found difficult. They are also terms which give us headaches today. Luke sees the redemptive significance of the cross differently. Jesus is the guide to life (*archegos tes zoes*). He goes before us. He opens up the way to us so that we can follow him on this way into the glory of God. The glory of God (*doxa theou*) is at the same time the form which God has made for himself of each of us. So Jesus' way is our way to the unique image which God has made for us. Jesus is the truly just man. If we look at him, we are put right, orientated on God, orientated on our dignity, made right by God.

The message that Luke wants to give to the Greeks and to us today is that Jesus is the saviour. Jesus has redeemed us through his death on the cross. But how are we to understand that? How can what happened on the cross then have a saving and redemptive effect for us? Two models of Greek thought help Luke to explain redemption through Jesus. One is the idea of drama. Luke depicts the way of Jesus as a drama. This drama comes to a climax in the death of Jesus on the cross: 'All those who had gathered for this drama and saw what had happened went home beating their breasts' (Luke 23.48). Drama was something that moved Greeks to the depths of their hearts. One doesn't watch a great play as an uninvolved spectator; one is drawn into it. The drama seeks to purge human emotions and passions. By depicting the heights and depths, the light and dark sides of human nature, and all the abysses of the soul, it leads to catharsis, to purification and purging. Drama changes people. When we look at the drama which Luke presents to us in his Gospel and above all in the passion narrative, we will be changed. Like those who saw it at the time, we will beat our breasts and be converted. We are to be moved in our hearts to go a new way, the way that really leads to life.

The second model that Luke uses to explain the healing and redemptive effect of the death of Jesus is the image of the just man. Jesus is the truly just man. The centurion doesn't confess that Jesus was Son of God (as in Matthew and Mark), but that 'he was truly a just man' (Luke 23.47). Luke wants to depict Jesus as the fulfilment of the Greek longing for the just man. In Greek philosophy the good, the beautiful, the seemly and the just are the characteristics of the true person. For Plato, justice is one of the prime cardinal virtues. It affects all parts of the soul and brings them together in harmony. Justice is the best constitution of the soul. The aim of justice is care of the soul. Jesus died on the cross a just man. He shows what a just man looks like, how the soul is constituted as well as it can be. And Jesus is the one who cares for our souls so that we have the courage to live rightly. In his dialogue *Gorgias*, Plato depicts his teacher Socrates as the model of justice. The just man doesn't mind being killed. Socrates compares himself to the physician who is accused by the cook because he gives the children bitter drinks to heal their wounds. Like Socrates, Jesus didn't just tell people what they wanted to hear. He is the physician who gives us medicines to heal our ailments. But he was accused by the cook, by people who were concerned only with themselves and their own well-being. When the centurion proclaims that Jesus is a just man, Luke is telling the Greeks. 'He is the truly just man for whom you have been waiting since Plato. He is the physician for your souls. If you look at him you yourselves will become just, orientated on God. Looking at Jesus on the cross will make you right, correct. He brings you into harmony with yourselves.' That is what redemption, liberation and healing mean for Luke.

The last supper

I want to give just a couple of examples of how Luke describes the passion of Jesus for Greek readers (and for us today), and attempts to make it understandable. It begins with the last supper, which Luke describes as a dinner with conversation at the table. For Luke this table-talk has the character of farewell discourses. As Jesus departs, he gives the disciples his last will and testament, just as Socrates proclaims his most important philosophical insights just before he dies by drinking hemlock. In this farewell meal Jesus once again shows the disciples his love. If elsewhere in his meals with sinners he has shown God's mercy, now his love culminates in his giving himself to the disciples in the signs of bread and wine. He has longed to eat this Passover meal with the disciples (Luke 22.15) and to leave behind the testimony of his love in the symbolic action of the broken bread and the cup. When the disciples come together as a community and break bread with one another, they recall Jesus' love; they can experience Jesus' love, which culminates for them in his surrender of himself on the cross.

After the meal the table-talk begins. The most important theme that Luke selects here is the theme of ruling and serving (Luke 22.24–7). Jesus as the Lord becomes the servant of the disciples, the *diakonos*, the one who waits on tables. The one who waits on tables serves life and makes possible for the community a joyful feast which evokes life and joy in those who celebrate it. In this saying Jesus expresses the essence of his mission. He isn't like the kings of the nations, who oppress others. He serves people so that they may enjoy God's gifts to the full. But his behaviour is now also to be a model for the disciples. They are not to strive to do others down so that they can believe in their own greatness. Jesus shows how all relations are turned upside-down: the leader becomes the servant, the greatest becomes the smallest. Jesus is the one who awakens in people the life that God has given them.

Then Jesus tells Peter to strengthen his brothers. That is his legacy to the disciples. The death of Jesus on the cross will challenge their faith. But Jesus prays for them, especially for Peter, who here appears as prototype of the disciples, that their faith may not fail. However, Peter must repent, be converted. Only then can he strengthen his brothers in the faith. Luke goes on to depict how Jesus himself is assailed and in prayer struggles to fulfil the will of God. Luke begins the scene on the Mount of Olives with the invitation to the disciples, 'Pray that you do not fall into temptation' (Luke 22.40). Only in prayer can Jesus resist his own temptation. And only prayer can strengthen the disciples in the many tribulations that they may expect. Jesus reaches his limits on the Mount of Olives. He senses that the way to the cross will ask too much of him in human terms. Jesus is confronted with his fear. He is in 'agony'. This agony is the last effort before the decisions and catastrophes that are about to begin. In his deadly agony sweat runs off his forehead 'like great drops of blood' (Luke 22.44). An angel from heaven appears to him and gives him new strength. Here Luke depicts Jesus as the model of the one who prays. Prayer is a matter of struggling with God. Without prayer we are hopelessly in the grip of our fears. Prayer gives us the power to resist the temptations and tribulations of our life. We aren't left alone in our prayer. God will send us, too, his angel, to support us and to give us new strength for our way.

Jesus' way to the passion

After praying Jesus is strengthened for going the way of his suffering. The way of the passion begins with his arrest. Luke takes over large parts of the Gospel of Mark in his passion narrative. Nevertheless he gives his description its own stamp. Jesus here is more active than he is in Mark. He addresses the one who has betrayed him, 'Judas, are you betraying the Son of man with a kiss?' (Luke 22.48). When one of his disciples cuts off the right ear of the high priest's servant, Jesus heals the man. Even in his suffering he is still the physician who tends the wounds of his opponents. In Luke the squad which take Jesus prisoner is a purely Jewish group. Luke has a tendency to trivialize the role of the Romans in the execution of Jesus and foist all the blame on the Jews. His purpose here is to make Christianity respectable in the Roman empire. Here the historian Luke is not being faithful to the facts, but is interpreting them his own way. Thus he makes an effort to depict what goes on in the high priest's house, the betrayal of Peter, and the mockery by the guards in a way which is exciting and illuminating for his readers. In all that Luke writes we detect the gifted writer who has a sense of dramatic and artistic structure.

The assembled Jews take Jesus to Pilate. Luke depicts Pilate, the brutal Roman procurator, as an understanding man. Luke wants to make the Roman governor a witness to Jesus' innocence. Only Luke depicts Jesus being sent on to Herod (Luke 23.6–12). Evidently he wants to cite Herod as well as Pilate as a witness to Jesus' innocence. He describes Herod as an educated Hellenistic man who is fascinated by interesting things, miracles and particularly learned sayings. But Jesus disappoints Herod's desire for miracles. He is silent. His silence is a sign of the servant of God and as such is comprehensible to Jewish readers. But the Hellenists, too, knew silence as a sign of divinity, for example in the cult of Mithras. Jesus' silence turns Herod's admiration into contempt and mockery. Herod is not an educated and wise man but someone who is interested only in sensations. His true nature comes out in the encounter with Jesus. As we look at the drama of the passion we are confronted with our own truth. We recognize who we really are. Our being becomes manifest. Herod shows his falsehood by dressing Jesus in a splendid white robe and sending him back to Pilate. On this day Herod and Pilate become friends.

Now Pilate calls together the high priests and the other leaders. He proclaims Jesus' innocence to all and also cites Herod as a witness to this innocence. But the Jewish crowd reacts by calling for the crucifixion of Jesus. Three times Pilate asserts Jesus' innocence. But the Jews dominate everyone with their cry. Luke avoids saying that Pilate actually pronounces the death sentence. Pilate simply gives way to the pressure of the crowd and hands Jesus over to the Jews. That certainly isn't historical. For only the Romans had the right to crucify people. Luke omits the mockery of Jesus by the Roman soldiers. He introduces the soldiers only at the cross.

On the way to the cross Jesus meets Simon of Cyrene and the weeping women (Luke 23.26–31). Again it is men and women who accompany Jesus on his way to the cross. Both serve as models. Just as Simon carries the cross behind Jesus, so too the disciples are to take the cross upon themselves and follow Jesus. Jesus addresses the weeping women: 'Daughters of Jerusalem, do not weep for me; weep rather for yourselves and your children' (Luke 23.28). Jesus doesn't want compassion but their repentance. This too is probably a warning to readers. When we read and meditate on the passion of Jesus we are not to dissolve into pity but to be converted and change our lives. The passion of Jesus is to change the way we think and act. It is meant to leave us changed and transformed. Jesus' death on the cross is the loudest warning to repent that he can give.

The crucifixion

Luke has once again constructed his account of the crucifixion skilfully. Here too he uses the stylistic means of polarity. Jesus is crucified between two criminals, one of whom is repentant and the other hardened. The cross of Jesus can lead us to repentance. But we can also look at it hard-heartedly. In that case it doesn't heal and redeem us. Jesus prays even on the cross. He prays for his execution-ers, 'Father, forgive them; they do not know what they are doing' (Luke 24.34). On the cross Jesus opens up the possibility of repentance for all men and women. Those who see Jesus' love even for his murderers may trust that they too will be forgiven. Thus the crucifixion of Jesus represents the ultimate consequences of God's forgiving love. In Luke's Gospel the cross doesn't bring about forgiveness but expresses it, and in this way communicates it to us sinners. Those who see Jesus' forgiving love know in their hearts that all their faults have been forgiven.

'The people stayed there watching' (Luke 23.35). Here the people are being shown a drama. The drama addresses their emotions and thus purges them. First the onlookers see how Jesus is mocked three times, by the leaders, by the soldiers and by the criminal on the left. This mockery is opposed by the confession of the criminal on the right: 'We deserved it; we are paying for what we did. But this man has done nothing wrong' (Luke 23.41). Then the man who is being crucified with Jesus asks Jesus to think of him when he comes into his kingdom. Jesus answers him: 'In truth I tell you, today you will be with me in paradise' (Luke 23.43). Here Jesus' merciful love is perfected on the cross. It offers everyone the chance of repentance, even in the hour of their death. And Jesus' promise to the criminal on the right is also a promise to us that in death we will be led by Jesus to paradise. In death the 'today' is perfected, the death of Jesus becomes pure presence for us and gives us the certainty that today with him we will enter God's glory.

Then Luke describes Jesus' death. Here again he becomes the historian. He gives the precise hour of death. But the indication of time is also meant symbolically. In the middle of the day the sun goes dark and darkness covers the whole land. Jesus doesn't die with a cry but with a prayer, 'Father, into your hands I commend my spirit' (Luke 23.46). While the trumpets sound out from the temple with their summons to evening prayer, Jesus prays with the words of Psalm 31. This prayer was the evening prayer of pious Jews. But Jesus prefaces the word of prayer in the psalms with his own way of addressing God, 'Abba'. In death he dies into the loving arms of his Father. He goes home to the Father whom he addresses with the tender, loving words 'Abba', 'dear father'. In this description Luke wants to show that for Jesus death is not terrible, but the consummation of love. What Jesus had already told the teachers in the temple as a child is fulfilled: 'Did you not know that I must be about my Father's business?' (Luke 2.49). Prayer takes Jesus through the gates of death into the loving arms of his Father. That is the promise that Luke sees in Jesus' dying. As we pray in death, we too will not fall into nothingness but into God's love. Jesus breathes his last. He gives back his spirit to his Father. Here too Luke again brings together Jewish and Greek elements. Jesus prays with the words of a Jewish psalm. But his death itself is described in the language of Luke's Hellenistic environment. Seneca described the death of Heracles in a similar way: 'Take my spirit, I pray you, to the stars . . . See, my father calls me and opens heaven. I come, father, I come.'

The reaction to Jesus' death

Luke now relates a threefold reaction to Jesus' death. The threefold mockery is followed by a threefold affirmation. First of all the Roman centurion praises God. So he sees God himself at work in the death of Jesus. He therefore praises God for this man. In contrast to Matthew and Mark, he doesn't confess that he was the Son of God, but 'Truly, this was a just man' (Luke 23.47). In a symposium Plato spoke of a person who is not as full of intrigues as we are, of someone who is truly just. He is driven out of the city and killed. This just man for whom the Greeks have longed is Jesus. But the Jews, too, see their desire for the messiah fulfilled in this just man. For the messiah is the righteous man whom God sends. When the centurion recognizes that Jesus is a just, a righteous man, God's glory is dawning on him. Here Luke is describing Jesus' relation-ship to God. He doesn't use the term Son of God, but describes the man Jesus in such a way that God dawns on the onlookers.

The second reaction comes from the crowd. We have been told that these people flocked to the drama. And they saw what happened. The history of Jesus is a drama: not a fictitious drama but a real one. But it has the same effect as a Greek play. The people 'went away beating their breasts' (Luke 23.48). They have repented. They have been con-verted. They have been moved. The death of the just man has transformed them. They go away from the drama changed. We too cannot look at the death of Jesus in a simply objective way. If we really meditate on it, if we really look at it, then it transforms us and we cannot go on living as we did. The Greeks experienced God essentially through seeing. When I see Jesus dying on the cross I see God, I see the heavens open. Thus the drama of the cross becomes the deepest part of my experience of God. As I look at this just man who hangs innocent on the cross and even prays for his murderers, God dawns on me. Heaven opens for me and the mystery of divine love becomes visible.

Luke attributes the third reaction to Jesus' death to all his acquaintances and the women who had followed Jesus 'since the time in Galilee' (Luke 23.49). It is said that they all stood there and saw everything. They stay by Jesus. They stay there, and do not flee in the face of his death. And they see everything. Here Luke doesn't use the Greek word *theorein*, used to describe watching a play, 'contemplate, consider', but *horan*, which means 'see, pay attention to, keep in view'. This is more a seeing with the senses which doesn't yet understand but keeps in view everything that makes the impact of what has happened go deep into the heart, until the heart understands what it has seen. And Luke once again talks of seeing. The women accompany Joseph of Arimathea, who takes the body of Jesus down from the cross and lays it in a rock tomb in which no one has yet been buried. The women 'took note of the tomb and how his body had been laid' (Luke 23.55). Here Luke uses the Greek word *etheasanto* = 'they looked, watched attentively, with wonderment'. This word is also used of spiritual seeing. It is a form of insight, understanding. The significance of the fact that Jesus is being laid in a rock tomb in which no one has yet been laid dawns on them. This burial in an untouched rock tomb has been said to be 'cultic'; the women see it as if they were involved in the Greek mystery cults. The women look at the untouched tomb and at the body of Jesus and they have an inkling that God will do something utterly new, something authentic and unprecedented. In the resurrection Jesus will rise into the clarity of God.

For Luke, Jesus' death is also a model for the way in which Christians die. Thus in the Acts of the Apostles he describes the death of Stephen in similar words to the death of Jesus. The mystery of Jesus dawns on Stephen just as he dies. 'But he, filled with the Holy Spirit, gazed into heaven and saw the glory of God, and Jesus sitting at God's right hand. "Look, I can see heaven thrown open," he cried, "and the Son of man standing at the right hand of God"' (Acts 7.55f.). That fills his sight. He no longer sees the man Jesus, but he sees heaven open and Jesus in his glory with God. Luke interprets the death of Jesus in the death of Stephen. Those who meditate on Jesus' death on the cross will see heaven open. And in them the confidence will grow that their vision will be fulfilled in their own deaths. Then they will truly see God, and in God Jesus. Jesus stands at the right hand of God. He is upright. He is risen and now stands always for us, so that we too may die good deaths. Stephen dies with the words, 'Lord Jesus, receive my spirit' (Acts 7.59). In our death we will be taken up by Jesus for ever into his fellowship with the Father.

9

Resurrection Stories

Luke is the only evangelist to tell us not only of the resurrection but also of the ascension of Jesus. Jesus has come down from heaven to travel with us men and women and to share our ways. In his death and his resurrection he returns to heaven. There he sits at the right hand of God and intercedes for us. And he sends us the Holy Spirit, in whose power we may do the same deeds as he did and bear the message of the kingdom of God to all the world. Luke develops two ideas above all in his message of the resurrection and ascension of Jesus: first he wants to describe how Jesus could not be held by death because he had been filled with God's spirit and was the Son of God. Secondly the notion of the ascension serves him to express the continuity of Jesus' activity. Jesus supports his disciples from heaven. He sends his Spirit to drive the disciples on, to proclaim the message of salvation to all the world, and to show people the way to life.

Psalm 16 as the grounds for the resurrection

Luke has developed his theology of the resurrection above all in Peter's speech at Pentecost. Peter accuses the Jews of having 'nailed to the cross and killed by the hands of lawless men' (Acts 2.23) Jesus, whom God had authenticated by miracles and signs: 'But God raised him to life, freeing him from the pangs of death; for it was impossible that he should be held fast by death' (Acts 2.24). And then Peter cites Psalm 16 as the grounds for the resurrection. The person who prays this psalm has God constantly before his eyes. The inner fellowship with God which he experiences gives him the certainty that this fellowship cannot be destroyed even by death. 'So my heart rejoiced, my tongue delighted; my body, too, will rest secure, for you will not abandon me to the underworld or allow your holy one to see corruption. You have taught me the way of life, you will fill me with joy in your presence' (Acts 2.26–8). Through the spirit with which he was filled, Jesus experienced such a deep fellowship with God that he could not fall away from it even in death. God himself raised him up. And so for us he has become the 'guide to life' (Acts 3.15). The term *archegos tes zoes* = 'guide to life, pioneer of life' has become a central concept of Luke's theology of the resurrection (Acts 3.15). Jesus will also lead those who are associated with him to life, to a life which cannot be destroyed even by death. In his theology of the resurrection Luke is above all concerned with the question of life. As the Risen One, Jesus leads us to real life. The task of the apostles consists in proclaiming 'words of life' (Acts 5.20). In the resurrection Jesus shows us 'the ways to life' (Acts

2.28). God has also given 'the repentance that leads to life' (Acts 11.18) to the Gentiles. A longing for life was not known only to the Greeks. It is just as topical today. What young people today long for above all is really to live, to live a fulfilled life. Life is the supreme good. Luke responds to this longing. Jesus is the guide to life. If we follow him, we will find life. Luke wanted to instil this message of the resurrection in the hearts of the Greeks. He also wants to proclaim it to us today, so that we don't run after false promises which bring us disappointment instead of life. Jesus the Risen One is the only one who can lead us to true life.

I shall now go briefly through the resurrection stories in the Gospel. Luke describes the encounter with the Risen Christ in his own way. He uses what he has before him. Here he is guided by the idea of Easter Day, which is made present every Sunday in the worship of the community. Luke sums up the Easter appearances in three images, and in them the mystery of Jesus Christ and his disciples. Whereas Matthew and Mark report the Easter experiences in Galilee, Luke makes them all take place in Jerusalem. Jerusalem is the place of the resurrection and the place from which the message of salvation goes out to all the world. In his three images of Easter Luke shows us how the resurrection could happen to us today. If we meditate on these images, the life to which the guide to life wants to lead us will dawn on us.

The women at the tomb

The first picture of Easter that Luke paints for us is the meeting between the women and the two angels of the resurrection at the empty tomb. The women find that the stone has been rolled away from the tomb. For us, resurrection means that the stone which blocks us has been rolled away, that the life in us is no longer sealed up. When the women go to the empty tomb in perplexity and do not find the body of Jesus there, two men in shining garments come to them and say: 'Why look among the dead for someone who is alive? He is not here: he has risen. Remember what he told you when he was still in Galilee: that the Son of man was destined to be handed over into the power of sinful men and be crucified, and rise again on the third day' (Luke 24.5–7). The angels address the women with a proverb. There is no point in seeking the living among the dead. Resurrection means life. Christ is alive. And one doesn't seek the living in the tomb. If we want to meet Jesus, the Risen One, we won't find him in the past, in dead letters or in rigid laws. We will meet him where there is life. Jesus wants to lead us to life. Our gaze must be directed forwards, and not backwards into the past. There is little point in disputing the correctness of these words. We are to trust the life that they seek to arouse in us.

In Mark the angel directs the women to Galilee. There they will meet the Risen Christ. In Luke the angels remind the women of the words that Jesus spoke to the disciples, both men and women, in Galilee. The empty tomb puts the sayings of Jesus in a new light. Resurrection means a new understanding of the words of Jesus. If we remind ourselves of the words which Jesus spoke during his life-time on the basis of his resurrection, the real mystery of Jesus will dawn on us. Easter is the key which opens up the meaning of the words of Jesus for us. The women remind themselves of the words of Jesus and understand them. Easter happens for them in a new understanding of the words. They return to Jerusalem and report to the disciples what they have seen and heard. But the disciples think that their words are women's gossip. This expression shows the offence felt by men who had to accept that women had the first experience of the resurrection and evidently also of faith in the Risen Christ.

The disciples on the road to Emmaus

Then Luke tells what is probably the finest Easter story, Jesus' meeting with the disciples on the road to Emmaus. Here the motif of travelling is taken up again. Jesus is the unknown traveller who goes along with two disillusioned disciples leaving the city of Jerusalem. The hope that they cherished hasn't been fulfilled. Jesus, whom they think to be a great prophet, has been crucified. But because they are still talking to each other about their disillusionment, the Risen Christ can enter into conversation with them and interpret their experiences in a different way. Here, too, resurrection means a new interpretation of the life of Jesus, but also a new interpretation of our own way through life. On our way we will often have the same experience as the disciples on the road to Emmaus. We will become disillusioned. The illusions that we had about life collapse. And sometimes we believe that we are 'powerful in action and speech before God and the whole people' (Luke 24.19). Then a line is drawn through our image of ourselves. Everything is taken out of our hands. We face the ruin of our life. What we would most like to do is to run away from it. But we aren't alone on our way. As long as we talk with one another, Jesus, the Risen One, will go with us and disclose the meaning of our life to us. The remark 'Was it not necessary for the messiah to suffer all this in order to enter into his glory?' (Luke 24.26) is the key to understanding Jesus' destiny, and also our own fate. It was God's will, which we cannot question, that the messiah should suffer in order to enter into his glory. And that is our way, too. Only through tribulations do we attain true life, the glory that God has prepared for us, in the form that God has devised for us. It is good that we have been disillusioned, that the images that we have made of ourselves have been shattered. Only in this way do we attain God's glory. Only in this way can we become the image that God has made of us.

Jesus interprets the whole of holy scripture to the two travellers. He shows them that the death and resurrection of Jesus are the summary of the whole Bible. That means not only that the death and resurrection of Jesus are foretold in some verses of the Bible. Rather, Luke understands by this that the whole message of the Bible can be summed up in the mystery of the death and resurrection of Jesus. All the sayings about the God who redeems and saves, the God who leads us out of the pit, who frees the enslaved people, who saves us from distress, reach their fulfilment in the death and resurrection of Jesus. There is nothing from which God cannot save us. God has raised Jesus from the dead. So God will also lead us from darkness into light, from the tomb to life, from rigidity to liveliness, from imprisonment to freedom, from blindness to sight, from paralysis to walking, from legalism to love. In the resurrection the meaning of holy scripture dawns on Luke. There he first recognizes what the comforting words of Isaiah mean: 'Should you pass through the waters I shall be with you; or through rivers, they will not swallow you up. Should you walk through fire, you will not suffer, and the flame will not burn you. For I, the Lord, am your God, I, the Holy One of Israel, am your saviour' (Isa. 43.2f.). There is no longer any darkness which is not penetrated by the light of Easter. There is no longer a tomb in which life is not already stirring.

The disciples ask Jesus to stay with them. 'It is nearly evening and the day is almost over' (Luke 24.29). That is an image of our life. Where darkness is coming over us, where the night falls on our soul, we may ask the Risen One to remain with us. Jesus stops with the two disciples. He becomes their guest so as to be with them. That is a picture not just of the resurrection, but also of the celebration of the eucharist. We encounter the Risen Christ in the celebration of the eucharist. There he is with us, there he talks to us, there he interprets scripture to us, and there the mystery of our life dawns on us. And then Luke describes the meal of the Risen Christ with the disciples in the words with which he has described the last supper. Jesus 'took the bread and said the blessing; then he broke it and handed it to them' (Luke 24.30). The eyes of the disciples are opened. They recognize him. But at the same moment he becomes invisible to them. *Aphantos* = 'invisible' is a typical expression from the Greek world. Jesus disappears from the gaze of the disciples. That is the mystery of the resurrection. The Risen Christ is with us and among us. He breaks the bread for us. In the celebration of the eucharist he encounters us, he becomes visible to us. But we can't keep hold of him with our eyes. For Luke resurrection essentially has to do with opening. Our heart opens (Acts 16.14), and so do our spirit (Luke 24.45) and our eyes (Luke 24.31). And the Risen Christ opens scripture to us; he discloses the meaning of holy scripture to us (Luke 24.31). In such openness we may see the Risen Christ. But the openness also means that we must let him go. He keeps disappearing from our gaze again. However, if the Risen Christ opens our heart, our spirit and our eyes, we burn in love for him. We are moved by the words and actions of Jesus to the depths of our heart. The burning of our heart drives us back towards our fellow men and women. So that same hour the disciples set out with burning hearts and return to Jerusalem to report their experience to the other disciples. The experience of the resurrection sends us on our way to tell others what we have seen and heard.

The appearance of Jesus to all the disciples

The third picture that Luke paints of the day of the resurrection is the appearance of Jesus to all the disciples. The disciples return from Emmaus to Jerusalem full of joy. The others, men and women, who have stayed at home tell them that the Lord has truly risen and appeared to Simon. While they are still talking about this, Jesus himself appears in their midst. They are terrified and afraid because they think that they're seeing a ghost. Jesus shows them his hands and feet: 'See by my hands and my feet that it is I myself. Touch me and see for yourselves; a ghost has no flesh and bones as you can see I have' (Luke 24.39). Here Luke wants to show the Greeks what resurrection means. The Greeks could imagine that the Risen Christ was spirit, that his soul had separated from his body and now existed by itself. But resurrection is more than that. The person of Jesus has risen, body and soul. With his reference to hands and feet Luke is responding to Platonic philosophy, which can only imagine the liberation of the soul from the prison of the body. Resurrection is resurrection of the body. It gives us hands which grasp life, touch people tenderly, make tender love possible. And resurrection puts us on our feet so that we stand up and go our way, the way that leads us to life.

The words 'It is I myself = *ego eimi autos*' are a reply to Stoic philosophy. In the Stoa, *autos* denotes the core of the person, the inner sanctuary of the human being, the inner sphere of the self in which God dwells in people. Luke often emphasizes the word *autos*. When he does, he is always pointing to the Lord. Christ is 'he himself'. Luke begins sentences with *kai autos* 43 times, whereas the phrase never occurs in Matthew, and in Mark only three times. Nor does Luke ever use it in the Acts of the Apostles. That shows that he restricts it to Christ. When the Risen Christ now says 'It is I myself', Luke is giving an answer to the longing of Stoic philosophy. In the Stoa people longed to be freed from the cares and needs of this world. They wanted to get through to their true selves, to the inner sanctuary in which no one could hurt them. For

Luke, resurrection means that Jesus has become 'he himself', that he is living out his self in all its purity. And for us, too, resurrection means becoming completely ourselves, free from the superficialities of everyday life, free from the power of others, their expectations and demands and verdicts, rising from the inauthentic to the authentic, entering the inner sanctuary in which God dwells in us and in which we come into contact with the unfalsified and untouched picture of God in us. For Luke, Jesus, the Risen One, is the model for our being ourselves, for our selfhood.

Jesus invites his disciples to touch him. Luke uses the Greek word *pselaphao* = 'feel, touch' once again, in Paul's speech on the Areopagus, in which Paul is deliberately responding to the philosophy of the Stoa. People are 'to seek God and, by feeling their way towards him, succeed in finding him; and indeed he is not far away from any of us' (Acts 17.27). With his 'touch me', Luke is indicating to the adherents of Stoic philosophy that people can touch God in Jesus Christ. In his hands and feet they can touch God himself. Doing that fulfils their longing for a God who can be experienced with the senses. In every eucharist we can touch Jesus in the bread that is put into our hands. In the early church Christians touched their ears and eyes with the body of Christ, not just to taste Christ but to touch him and be touched by him in a tender way.

Finally Jesus accepts some food and eats with his disciples. He has a meal with them. Resurrection creates a new community. At the meals that the disciples have together, the Risen Christ himself is in their midst. For Luke, the eucharist is always an experience of the Risen Christ. The intimacy and the joy expressed in his depiction of the Easter meal should also shape our celebration of the eucharist. Jesus discloses the scriptures to his disciples, men and women, and shows himself to them as God and man, as the one who has become his true self, so that we may rise from inauthenticity into authenticity, from rigidity into liveliness, and from isolation into a new togetherness.

Now Luke concludes his Gospel with a farewell speech by Jesus, with his testament. Jesus reminds the disciples once again of all the words that he spoke when he was 'with them'. He opens their minds (*nous*) to understand scripture and once again he sums up the mystery of his life. His life and suffering, his death and resurrection, are the fulfilment of the whole of holy scripture. With the word 'fulfilment', 'consummation', Luke indicates that Jesus' death and resurrection sum up all God's action described to us in the Bible. The death and resurrection of Jesus show us that there is nothing that God cannot use and change. There is no death that cannot be transformed into life, no darkness that cannot become bright, no fear that cannot become trust, no comfortlessness that cannot be comforted. Death and resurrection tell us that everything can be transformed. Nothing can separate us from God. God is present everywhere, even in death, in the tomb, in solitude, in darkness, in despair.

Luke tells us that it is also said in scripture that in the name of Jesus a proclamation is made to all peoples that 'they are to repent, so that their sins are forgiven' (Luke 24.47). It is remarkable that Luke understands this as the good news that the disciples are to proclaim to all the world. Conversion as a presupposition for the forgiveness of sins seems to have nothing to do with the fate of Jesus. That is a universal human message. But this message is to be proclaimed in the name of Jesus. Because Jesus has attained resurrection through death, all people have the opportunity to be converted and thus have their sins forgiven. Looking at Jesus they are to repent, to see behind things, so that they recognize the real truth of their lives. Repentance leads to forgiveness. For Luke, forgiveness means reorientating our lives on God, no longer falling short of our goal, but succeeding in our lives. The disciples have the task of proclaiming forgiveness, this fulfilled life, to all peoples. For this the Risen Christ sends them his spirit, 'the power from on high' (Luke 24.49). The 'radiance from on high' (Luke 1.78) has already visited us in the birth of Jesus. Now the Risen Christ fills us with 'power from on high' so that we bear the light of Christ to all the world. In the disciples' preaching, Jesus' influence spreads in the world and permeates the history of humankind more and more.

Luke ends his Gospel with the account of the ascension. And he begins the Acts of the Apostles with the same event. There is a contradiction here. In the Gospel Jesus ascends to heaven on Easter Day, but in Acts he ascends only on the fortieth day after the resurrection. This contradiction indicates that Luke wants to make a theological statement. The history of Jesus began with prayer in the temple and it ends with the praise of the disciples in the temple. Luke ends the Gospel with a liturgy. In the Gospel he interprets the ascension cultically, whereas in Acts he interprets it ecclesiastically and historically. In the Gospel the ascension takes place so to speak in a liturgical festival.

In the Acts of the Apostles Luke describes the process of the ascension. The forty days are an image of human time. The forty days as the time of transformation after Jesus' resurrection are no longer marked by fasts and the experience of the wilderness, but by the appearances of Jesus. The risen Christ goes with us until we too are taken up into heaven.

Jesus bids farewell to his disciples with the great blessing. After being given this blessing they return to Jerusalem full of joy. 'They were constantly in the temple praising God' (Luke 24.53). This reflects the worship of the community, which is stamped with joy and praise. The life, death, resurrection and ascension of Jesus have their effect on the disciples in this attitude of joy and praise. Jesus has already brought joy by his birth. This joy is fulfilled in his resurrection and ascension. Joy (Greek *chara*) is our reaction to the *charis* = 'grace' that is given to us in Jesus. Luke has understood Jesus' activity to be one of illuminating our hearts, making the glory of God shine again in us, banishing all the oppression, fear and darkness from our hearts. In joy the heart expands. It experiences the breadth and freedom of the resurrection. That is reason enough for praising God. Joy is expressed in praise, and at the same time praise increases the joy in our hearts, so that it increasingly permeates and transforms body and soul.

10

What Are We To Do?

Luke doesn't just want to enthuse readers about Jesus. Those who understand Jesus must also change their lives. The history of Jesus goes on in the disciples, who change the world by a new form of behaviour. The spirit of God has an effect on history not only through words but also through a new way of doing things. Today we've become allergic to a moralizing spirituality. But Luke never raises a moralizing finger. He doesn't preach morality but tells stories which touch our hearts and make us ask, 'What shall we do?' He doesn't theorize about the relationship between love of God and love of neighbour but gives two examples to illustrate specifically how we can love our neighbour today without wearing ourselves out in the process: the example of the Good Samaritan (Luke 10.30–8) and the example of Mary and Martha (Luke 10.38–42). The priest and the Levite who are preoccupied with worshipping God in the cult pass by the man who has fallen victim to robbers. The Samaritan has compassion on him. He 'went up to him and bandaged his wounds, pouring oil and wine on them. He then lifted him on to his own mount and took him to an inn and looked after him' (Luke 10.34). Here

Luke paints a picture of true humanity. The parable describes Jesus himself as the Good Samaritan. This is the most authentic self-portrait that Jesus has painted of himself. But at the same time the parable challenges the reader to act like Jesus. Luke is a practical theologian. He has no interest in theoretical discussions. Concrete action shows whether someone has understood the message of Jesus and is living it out. We fulfil the words of Jesus when we do something that the situation requires of us, when our eyes aren't closed to people who have fallen among robbers and lie wounded by the wayside.

But Luke knows the danger of wearing ourselves out by helping others in order to soothe our bad conscience. We think that we have to save the whole world. We're torn between our bad conscience, which urges us to help, and our inability to help everyone. So as a counterbalance to a lofty ideal of helping Luke produces the story of Mary and Martha (Luke 10.38–42). Martha is the hospitable woman who busies herself with looking after guests. Hospitality was highly valued in the ancient world. So what Martha does is good and gives people pleasure. But she is blind to the needs of her guests. She thinks that Jesus and his disciples primarily want to be well looked after. She doesn't notice at all how she is putting her own needs above Jesus. She doesn't listen to him, doesn't discover what he really needs and what he wants. Her harsh criticism of her sister Mary, who simply sits at Jesus' feet and listens to what he has to say, shows that her help isn't completely unselfish. Her sensitivity indicates that by what she does she wants to draw attention to herself and to receive praise. She wants to show that she is more hospitable than other women. She

isn't concerned with the actual moment but with after-
wards, with the good reputation that she will get through
her actions. And perhaps she is also concerned about her
bad conscience, which she wants to ease by the help she
offers. Some people hide behind a great deal of work,
however meaningful and helpful to people it may be, in
order to protect themselves against any criticism. They
stop asking themselves questions, listening to what God
really wants of them.

Mary and Martha represent two poles in us. Each of us
has a Mary and a Martha inside us. And in us, too, the
Martha is usually louder. She has the better arguments.
She has something to show. She does something. She fulfils
God's will: hospitality. So Jesus has to defend Mary. In us
too, the slight suspicion that we are simply giving way to
the moment, that we are sitting in the presence of Jesus
and without any ulterior aim listening to what he has to
say to us, is also suppressed by the louder voices which call
on us to help the many sufferers. Jesus reinforces the gen-
tle voice which speaks to us on our Mary side: 'Mary has
chosen the better part, and it is not to be taken from her'
(Luke 10.42). It's good to keep quiet and listen in the
silence to what Jesus wants to say to us now at this
moment. Those who are always thinking only of the future
and their reputations miss out on life – on God and themselves. In Luke's language, for Mary to sit at Jesus' feet
means that she is the pupil and disciple of Jesus, on the
same footing as the men. So Mary breaks out of the one-
sided role of the caring and hospitable woman. Just like
men, women are called to go to school with Jesus as disciples and then likewise to preach the good news.

Attitudes to possessions and riches

Luke practises another way of suggesting a new relationship to the disciples by telling parables. The parables are often about the question 'What shall I do?' This is the question which the rich farmer (Luke 12.17) and the unjust steward ask (Luke 16.3). These parables are about how to deal rightly with possessions. For the Greek Luke this is an important topic. Luke is the evangelist of the poor. More than any other evangelist, he focuses on the topics of poverty and riches, possessions and the renunciation of possessions, communal sharing and social obligation. Luke himself probably came from the well-to-do middle class. But evidently he has a strong social conscience. For him it is important for Christians not to hang on to their possessions but to share them with the poor. Those who gather riches only for themselves have neither understood Jesus' intentions nor do they know about the mystery of human life, which is bounded by death. Those who take their human existence seriously know that it is impossible to gather any lasting treasures in this life. Material wealth perishes with death. So it is important to be rich before God. That happens in love, which is expressed practically by sharing possessions. Stories like that of the rich farmer (Luke 12.13–21) are told from Seneca to Hofmannsthal, from the book of Jesus Sirach to Lucian of Samosata. In Lucian the money-maker Gniphon in the underworld has to watch his hard-earned money being squandered in a very short time by the dissolute Rhodochoris. The theme of sharing possessions is as modern today as it was then. Christians are not to fall victim to the greed of those who speculate on the stock market; they are to become rich before God (Luke 12.21). True riches lie in us. The treasure is in our soul. It is the love that flows from us. But that love will flow only if our money also flows, if we share our possessions.

Among the Gentile Christian readers of the Gospel of Luke there will certainly have been many merchants who had accumulated some wealth. Acts talks of Lydia, who dealt in purple. In his Gospel Luke thinks of the material prosperity which comes about through investments and through selling and trading. The well-to-do classes of the population included big landlords, big businessmen and those who had contracts to collect taxes. Luke is concerned above all with the effect of wealth on human behaviour. People can make riches an ideal; wealth leads to avarice and ambition. The rich man is caught up in earthly cares and enjoyments. He forgets God. For the evangelist there are two attitudes which stamp the way in which Christians deal with the goods of this world: first sharing possessions, and secondly being carefree and having an inner freedom in dealing with possessions (Luke 12.22–32). Those who are over-anxious about whether they have enough to eat and to wear are attaching too much importance to externals. Instead of being anxious about themselves, people should trust in God. God looks after them. Christians are to be concerned about the kingdom of God, about God ruling in them, God dwelling in their souls. God is the true treasure. 'Where your treasure is, there your heart is also' (Luke 12.32). Only if our heart rests in God does it become free of earthly care. Only if people have their foundation in God can they let go of their possessions and give gifts to the poor.

Luke knows yet another attitude towards possessions: faithfulness in the stewardship of earthly goods. 'Anyone who is trustworthy in little things is trustworthy in great; anyone who is dishonest in little things is dishonest in great' (Luke 16.10). Trustworthiness and faithfulness in the administration of earthly gifts is the presupposition for dealing well with God's spiritual gifts. God's real gift is salvation, is God himself, who gives himself to men and women in Jesus. 'If you are not trustworthy with what is not yours, who will give you what is your very own?' (Luke 16.12). The possessions that people have don't belong to them. They belong to God. What is our very own, what fits us, what corresponds to our nature, is the salvation that God gives us in Jesus.

Luke sees the reality of this world. He doesn't denounce possessions and money. But he calls for social behaviour. Those who have riches must sell what they have and give the proceeds to the poor. Jesus' demands were realized in the first community of disciples in Jerusalem. The gifts of the earth belong to all: 'And all who shared the faith owned everything in common; they sold their goods and possessions and distributed the proceeds among themselves according to what each one needed' (Acts 2.44f.). In his description of the sharing of goods in the earliest church Luke combines Greek Hellenistic ideals with Old Testament/Jewish promises. He isn't pursuing any romantic ideal of poverty; rather, he is concerned with the social obligation that goes with possession, with sharing possessions so that everyone has enough. This ideal, which the earliest church realized, is also in the evangelist's mind for his own time. It is an ideal which also attracts the Greeks;

it translates the sayings of Jesus about selling all possessions into the situation of the Greek traders and merchants
and shows them a way of following Jesus without giving up
their professions. In this way they can find true freedom
and real life as disciples of Jesus. Modern liberation theology therefore rightly refers to Luke. It translates Luke's
message for our time. In future, world peace will above all
depend on a right balance of possessions. So Luke's translation of the message of Jesus is highly topical today, not
only for the ethics of individuals but also for international
politics.

Repentance

'Repent' is one important answer that Luke gives to the
question 'what are we to do?' It is the answer that Peter
gives after his Pentecost sermon when his hearers ask,
'What are we to do, brothers?' 'You must repent and every
one of you must be baptized in the name of Jesus Christ
for the forgiveness of your sins, and you will receive the
gift of the Holy Spirit' (Acts 2.37f.). The Greek word for
repentance, *metanoia*, really means 'change one's mind,
think differently, see behind things'. For the Greeks,
repentance begins with thinking. Our thinking leads us
astray. If we have the wrong idea about ourselves and the
situation around us, we won't do justice to reality in our
behaviour either. We can behave rightly only if we see the
world rightly. However, we often see it only through the
spectacles of our projections. Therefore Luke's Jesus wants
to train his hearers to see reality rightly and to assess it
appropriately. Two passages should make that clear.

In Luke 12.54–6 Jesus refers his hearers to observations of the weather. When clouds rise in the west a good observer of the weather can conclude that rain is on the way. 'And when the wind is from the south you say that it's going to be hot, and it is. Hypocrites! You know how to interpret the face of the earth and the sky. How is it that you do not know how to interpret these times?' (Luke 12.55–6). People can interpret nature rightly, but they have no eyes for the meaning of history. They deliberately close their eyes to it. Jesus warns us to direct our attention to the specific events of our time, to assess them rightly and to react to them with appropriate behaviour. *Metanoia*, seeing the other, new thinking, will also lead to new behaviour.

Luke shows how we are to assess historical facts in the scene in Luke 13.1–9. In it people tell him the latest news, which includes incomprehensible political catastrophes and strokes of fate. Pilate massacred Galileans who wanted to offer sacrifice. The tower of Siloam fell down and killed eighteen people. 'Do you suppose that these Galileans were worse sinners than any others, that this should have happened to them? They were not, I tell you. No, but unless you repent you will all perish as they did' (Luke 13.2f.). Jesus may take up the theology of the Pharisees, who see every accident as a punishment for sins. But he doesn't confirm it. Instead of entering into a theological discussion as to why things happened like this, he turns his attention to the ones telling these news stories. They aren't about others but about ourselves. We will perish likewise unless we repent. Our lives will fail if we don't change our way of thinking .We aren't to ask why catastrophes happen but to understand them as questions put to us. We are asked what we live by. What meaning does our life have? We have no guarantee that we will reach a ripe old age. We can't take it for granted that our lives will work out. If they are to work out we need to repent. Repentance primarily means becoming aware that we are alienated from God, that our thought is passing God by. And then it means seeing our lives in God's light of God, understanding them in this light, seeing behind things and recognizing that God is the real destination and support for our lives. However, repentance isn't just seeing and knowing, but also deciding. It is a matter of deciding to live differently, to live in accordance with God's will and our own natures.

Zacchaeus, an example of repentance bringing joy

Luke wouldn't be a storyteller if he contented himself with reporting only Jesus' admonitions to repentance. He tells us the marvellous story of the conversion of one individual. This is the story of Zacchaeus, the chief tax collector (Luke 19.10). Zacchaeus was very rich, but short in stature. One could say that precisely because he was small and felt small, he attempted to compensate for his feelings of inferiority by earning as much money as possible. He did that by extorting it from people, as tax collectors did at that time: each of them got a contract to collect taxes for the Romans and they then exploited this for their own ends. Zacchaeus' wealth serves to heighten his feelings of self-worth. But he doesn't succeed here. The more money he accumulates, the more he is rejected by the Jews. That is the vicious circle in which many people with inferiority complexes end up. The more they want to stand out in order to gain recognition, the more they are isolated and rejected. Zacchaeus was a chief tax collector. He could believe in his greatness only if he did others down. He had to set himself above people, because he seemed too small alongside them. Putting yourself above people makes you lonely. And Zacchaeus can't get out of the vicious circle of loneliness and rejection by his own efforts. He needs the encounter with Jesus in order to be able to live differently, in order to repent.

It is interesting how many verbs Jesus uses here. Jesus enters the city and goes through it. Zacchaeus runs in front of the crowd. Evidently he can't get through it. He climbs a sycamore tree in order to be able to see Jesus. Jesus looks up to Zacchaeus. Previously everyone has been looking down on him or overlooking him. For the first time Zacchaeus feels human. In the Hellenistic milieu *anablepo* means looking up to heaven and to disembodied ideas. Jesus looks up to a *person*. He sees heaven in people. He sees the face of God in people. That makes Zacchaeus a new man. He gets a new face. He discovers his face in the face of Jesus. And his face is filled with joy. Jesus calls him by his name. Zacchaeus quickly comes down. This little man who wanted to rise high and therefore got beyond himself, comes down. He becomes humble, one with the earth. There on level ground the miracle of his transformation takes place. The man Zacchaeus is transformed by the man Jesus, who wants to celebrate with him, eat and drink with him. In this man Jesus, Zacchaeus experiences God's salvation. The experience changes him. Jesus doesn't preach repentance but lets Zacchaeus experience his love, which accepts people unconditionally. The experience of this love leads the chief tax collector to repent. He spontaneously offers to give half his possessions to the poor and repay fourfold what he has collected unfairly. Because he knows that he has been accepted, because he has come into contact with his own dignity, he no longer needs the mechanism of standing out from the rest and accumulating money. Now he is free to give what he had clung on to. The repentance takes place out of the experience of loving care and joy that radiate from his face. Those who read this story get new faces, like Zacchaeus. They rejoice because today Jesus looks at them and calls them by name. Their faces, which previously had looked only in the mirror, open up, and they see people as they are. They notice them and become their brothers and sisters. Instead of calling for repentance, this marvellous story actually makes repentance take place. That is Luke's user-friendly theology. Luke can dispense with doing people down, constantly reminding them of their sinfulness. He tells of the loving kindness of Jesus who encounters people in such a way that they repent joyfully and in this way discover their own humanism, their own humanity and loving-kindness.

A new way of dealing with sinners

Those who have repented themselves deal differently with sinners. They will not project their guilt on others and misuse them as scapegoats. Rather, they will deal with them as lovingly as Jesus did. The basis for Jesus' concern for sinners lies in the trust that sinners in particular are open to the good news of the merciful love of God. Luke portrays Jesus as someone who turns to sinners and eats and drinks with them. He tells a marvellous story, a prime example of his skill in creating scenes, the story of the encounter of Jesus with the woman who was a sinner (Luke 7.36–50). In this story, which stands out for its aesthetic qualities, Luke has used the stylistic means of the Greek symposium literature – above all the motif of the appearance of uninvited guests and the dialogue which is controlled by the Greek host.

Jesus is reclining – as was customary in Hellenistic circles – at table in the house of a Pharisee. Then the surprise happens. A woman who was well known as a sinner enters and approaches Jesus from behind. She moistens his feet with her tears, wipes them with her hair and anoints them with precious oil. Whereas anointing the head was part of the ritual of receiving guests at that time, anointing the feet was quite unprecedented. This is an erotic scene. For only his own wife or daughter may anoint a man's feet. And Jews felt that loosening the hair was especially erotic. The woman even kisses Jesus' feet. While the Pharisees are being furious about this woman, Jesus interprets her behaviour positively. He sees her tears, her distress, her longing for true love. He takes the initiative and perplexes the Pharisee who has been foremost in complaining about Jesus' reactions with a parable taken from the world of ancient banking practices (Luke 7.41f.). Then he publicly criticizes the Pharisee's behaviour and defends the woman's action. He sees the woman's action as an expression of her love. This love is a sign that much has been forgiven her. Jesus publicly promises the woman forgiveness in the presence of all the guests. Luke deliberately leaves the reader uncertain whether Jesus is forgiving the woman because she has shown him so much love or whether he is merely confirming the forgiveness which was the reason for her love. Forgiveness and love are interwoven. And it isn't worth arguing over which came first, the forgiveness or the love. Love and forgiveness are intertwined.

In this scene Luke doesn't just want to depict Jesus' loving care for the sinner. He certainly also has the situation of his community in view. Presumably there were plenty of 'Pharisees' among the Christians who turned up their noses at new converts with a dishonourable past. People who have been converted from a particularly difficult situation often show particular warmth. Their love is an expression of the forgiveness that they have experienced. Those who experience forgiveness as liberation from a failed life will now also forgive others with all their hearts. They won't lord it over sinners because they know that their own lives went wrong before forgiveness brought them on the new way of salvation. Like Stephen, they will forgive their murderers and in doing so imitate Jesus' example.

That Luke writes so much about sinners (cf. Luke 15) and so often mentions the forgiveness of sins as the central aspect of salvation (Acts 2.38) doesn't mean that he has a pessimistic view of humanity. Human beings aren't intrinsically bad. They have a nucleus of good. But often enough they lose sight of themselves and the truth about themselves. Sinners are those whose lives go wrong, who miss the mark and therefore condemn and reject themselves. When they repent and are baptized in the name of Jesus, they experience the forgiveness of their sins and receive the Holy Spirit. They experience an unconditional justification of their existence and a power in themselves which keeps them from continually lapsing into the same pattern of sin. That is a message that the Greeks could very well understand. They are constantly concerned with the question of the right way. How do I find my way? What way leads to life? Sin leads us on the wrong way. We miss the mark. The encounter with Jesus opens up a way along which our life works out. In our encounter with Jesus we are freed from the mistakes of our life story and filled with the Holy Spirit. The Holy Spirit enables us to live differently, to live as Jesus lived before us.

According to the Gospel of Luke Jesus did not atone for our sins by his death or wash them away. He promised God's forgiveness in a new way and endorsed it and sealed it through his life. According to Luke, Jesus has given us all a new understanding of ourselves, a new view of our lives. Luke's good news is that Jesus himself opens our eyes so that we can see ourselves and the world differently. Repentance, rethinking the new perspective that Jesus has given us, constitute this new self-understanding. We needn't make great efforts to repent. Jesus makes it possible for us to repent if we meet him today in the stories about him, as people met him then. And in the Holy Spirit he gives us the power to take other ways and to act differently in the light of this new perspective. We don't need any laborious programme of self-help of the kind offered in many books today. The Spirit itself urges us to go the 'new way', the way to true life. Those who take the new way that Jesus has opened up will find fulfilment.

Luke as the Evangelist of the Church's Year

The Gospel of Luke has made an impact on church history not only by the new ethic that Luke gives us but also by the spiritual approach that it invites us to take. This spiritual approach is shaped above all by personal prayer. But it also affects our liturgy, which makes what happened to Jesus present for us today. In the liturgical tradition Luke is regarded as the theologian of the church's year. There are various reasons for this. First, Luke begins his Gospel in the temple. While Zechariah is serving as a priest in the temple he receives the promise that he will have a son. And Luke ends his Gospel with the praise of the disciples in the temple: 'They were constantly in the temple praising God' (Luke 24.53). In this closing sentence to his Gospel, Luke has the worship of the community in view. In worship the community celebrates the memory of the mighty deeds that God has done in Jesus. What happened then becomes present in its celebration.

Luke depicts the activity of Jesus as a year of salvation. He thinks of Jesus being active for one year. Jesus understands his task as being 'to proclaim the Lord's year of grace' (Luke 4.19). This year of salvation that God has given us in Jesus Christ is repeated in the course of the church's year, so that it becomes ever more deeply embedded in history. Most festivals in the course of the church's year go back to Luke, like 24 June as the festival of John the Baptist and 25 December as the day of Jesus' birth (Luke 1.26). The period from Christmas to Candlemas is based on the story of the birth of Jesus as it is handed down to us by Luke. Passiontide, Easter, the Ascension of Christ and Pentecost have their foundation in the Gospel of Luke. And Luke has given the church more than the festivals and their chronological dependence on one another. On the basis of his Gospel Greek theologians developed a special theology of the church's year. Two notions are particularly important: Luke's theology of history and his understanding of drama.

A theology of history

As a Greek, Luke understands history as the place where God appears to human beings: *kai egeneto*, 'and it happened', is the phrase that Luke loves most. Jesus' life was an event, a historical event. What happens is significant for people. It moves them. It brings about salvation and redemption in them. What happened then is time and again made present in worship. Memory transposes the acts of God in history for those who take part in the liturgy in the present. The people who recall the history of Jesus in worship are inwardly moved and transformed by this history. As the history of Jesus is time and again commemorated in the course of the church's year, it is constantly embedded in world history and becomes established. In this way the redemption which came about in Jesus' year of salvation works itself out in human beings and reaches all generations. Human beings are essentially historical. They develop their nature in history. They are always shaped by history. They become themselves only by referring back to history. Luke takes the historicity of human beings seriously. Redemption, too, takes place in history and is worked out in history. Luke is familiar with the Greek philosophy of history, for which the results of an action in history are always part of the history. Remembrance and recollection are the two ways in which an event has an influence on history and on our historical being. The commemoration of the salvation history which comes to a climax in Jesus makes the past present, so that we can be affected by its claim. Remembrance internalizes what has happened so that it shapes the human heart. In this way redemption through Jesus Christ reaches us today.

The sevenfold 'today'

The way in which Luke seven times uses the word 'today' makes clear to us that what happened then happens to us today when we celebrate the liturgy. In narrating the most important events in the life of Jesus Luke says that 'today' salvation has come to people. The first 'today' interprets the birth of Jesus. The angel proclaims to the shepherds, 'Today is born to you in the city of David the saviour; he is the messiah, the Lord' (Luke 2.11). Today the fulfilment of the Old Testament promise of a messiah who will free the people is taking place. At the baptism of Jesus the voice from heaven (according to the Western manuscripts – that is probably the original text of Luke) proclaims, 'You are my son, today I have fathered you' (Luke 3.22). In his baptism Jesus is confirmed as the Son of God and receives the Holy Spirit, so that now he goes his way in the power of the Spirit, heals the sick and performs God's deeds. In his inaugural sermon in the synagogue of Capernaum Jesus himself proclaims, 'This text is being fulfilled today even while you are listening' (Luke 4.21). With the appearance of Jesus the year of salvation has dawned. Today what Jesus had promised is being fulfilled before people's eyes. Good news is brought to the poor, release is proclaimed to the captives, sight to the blind, and the oppressed are liberated. People are overwhelmed when the paralysed man is healed: 'They praised God and were filled with awe, saying, "We have seen incredible things today"' (Luke 5.26). 'Today' is mentioned twice in connection with Jesus' meal with the tax collector Zacchaeus and his friends: 'I am to stay at your house today' (Luke 19.5). And when Zacchaeus is transformed in his heart by Jesus' loving care and promises to give half his possessions to the poor, Jesus says to him, 'Today salvation has come to this house' (Luke 19.9). Jesus uses the last 'today' at the crucifixion of Jesus. When the criminal asks Jesus to think of him when he comes into his kingdom, Jesus replies, 'In truth I tell you, today you will be with me in paradise' (Luke 23.43). We could compare this sevenfold 'today' in the Gospel of Luke with the seven sacraments. In them, what happened at that time in and through Jesus happens to us today. Today we are reborn, today we are anointed with the Holy Spirit, today our guilt is forgiven, today our ailments are healed, today Jesus celebrates a meal with us and shows us his goodness and loving-kindness. Today we experience in celebrating the death and resurrection of Jesus that already we have been transported to paradise, that we are already participating in the glory of the Risen Christ.

So the most important stages in Jesus' life are associated with the word 'today'. This 'today' is comprehensible to both the Jews and the Greeks. Psalm 95.7 says, 'Today if you hear his voice'. The God who has spoken to the Israelites in the past speaks to us 'today' in the liturgy so that we do not harden our hearts but allow ourselves to be transformed by the word of God. But the 'today' is also familiar to the Greeks. In the celebration of the nocturnal mysteries the priest calls out to those celebrating, 'Today the virgin has given birth to light.' The mystery cults knew a 'today'. In the cult they celebrated what happened 'at that time', so that it might happen 'today' among us and move us. In their cult the Greeks sought to be connected to the holy time in which the gods performed their deeds. For them worship was the place at which the pure and holy time of the beginning, the creation of the world, was made present again, and profane time with its impurities was replaced. Those who recalled themselves in the liturgy of the holy time, the time of salvation, were as it were reborn. They began their existence once again with a full store of living power, as at the moment of their birth. A nostalgia for origins, a nostalgia for paradise, was the motivation for the Greeks in their festivals and celebrations. They longed to go back to the strong, fresh and pure world which existed at that time. They had a thirst for the holy and a longing for being. When the early Christians heard 'today' in the liturgy they knew that Christ himself was present

among them. They took part in the Lord's year of salvation. What moved people so much then, what transformed
them in their hearts and healed their wounds, happens to
them today. They share in the healing and liberating activity of Jesus. Jesus speaks to them today; today he touches
their blind eyes and their leprous bodies. With this theology of 'today' Luke shows us a way of bridging the deep
ditch of history and experiencing the event of Jesus today
as salvation and redemption.

A theology of drama

The second notion with which Luke enriches a theology
of the church's year is the Greek notion of drama. The
Greeks loved drama. In drama human conflicts were
depicted with all the emotions and passions that surfaced
in them. In them human beings became manifest in their
polarity between good and evil, light and darkness. Drama
brings spectators into contact with their own repressed
emotions and passions. They discover the abysses of their
heart, they recognize their needs and longings, their dangers and their inner divisions. For the Greeks drama pro-
duced a catharsis; in other words, the drama purged the
spectators of their inner pollutions by its passions and
emotions. When I go to see a great play I am inwardly
transformed. My emotions become clear and I come into
contact with my original self, with the pure image that
God has made of me. Luke described the life of Jesus as a
drama which moves spectators and changes them. And it
was natural for the first Christians time and again to present this drama in the liturgy, so that as at that time people

would go home beating their breasts. The early church fathers who developed a theology of the liturgy were mainly Greeks. They took up the idea of drama that they found on the one hand in Luke and on the other in the mystery cults practised in their environment. It would be good for us to allow ourselves to be inspired by the theology of drama today. Then our worship would be more inviting. And it would present the story of Jesus to those taking part in the liturgy in such a way that they are moved as the readers of Luke's Gospel were then. Even those who rarely go to church are still attracted by Luke's language when, for example, the story of the birth of Jesus is read out at a Christmas service, or when the parable of the prodigal son or the Emmaus story are among the readings.

Luke and liturgical prayer

In his Gospel Luke has given the church three prayer psalms which are sung daily in the liturgy in our monastic community and in many other places: the Benedictus in the morning, the Magnificat in the evening and the Nunc Dimittis at night. For me these three hymns express Luke's art in combining the past with the present and the future. In these hymns we praise God for what he did for us then and what he is doing for us today. We use these words every day and at the various festivals. They do not just describe what happened at the birth of John or at Christmas. Rather, the words are open to describe the mystery of any feast, whether this is Easter or Pentecost, the Ascension of Christ or a feast of Mary or one of the saints. They are always about God's gracious action to us today when we celebrate the liturgy.

Luke deliberately puts Zechariah's song of praise, which is really a poem of congratulation on the birth of John the Baptist, before the birth of Jesus. Thus Luke sees these words as an expression of the mystery of the incarnation which we reflect on afresh every morning. In Jesus God has visited us human beings. God becomes our guest. And as a gift he brings redemption with him. This redemption is described as deliverance from the hands of our enemies, as mercy which he shows us, making it possible for us to live without fear 'in holiness and righteousness before him all the days of our life' (Luke 1.75). And the birth of Jesus is celebrated as a visitation of radiant light from on high. In Christ the sun of salvation appears to us. It shines on us as we sit in darkness and the shadow of death, so that our steps are guided into the way of peace (Luke 1.79). The image of the shining star from heaven is familiar to Jews and Greeks. Christ is the figure of heavenly light. He is the true morning star which rises in our hearts. The church sings this song of praise every morning to confess that the rising sun points to Christ. What we observe in nature is an image of Christ as the true sun. Christ today brings us the light that drives away our darkness and makes it possible for us to take the way of peace.

The Magnificat is sung every day in the evening liturgy of Vespers. It is Mary's song of praise. In it Mary celebrates not only what God has done for her but God's activity in history and God's action in Jesus Christ, which turns all this world's standards upside down. In Jesus God has turned the balance of power in this world upside down.

Luke composes Mary's song of praise from Jewish prayers. It has similarities to Pharisaic psalms. But at the same time he alludes to Greek motifs. The turning of things upside down is also a well-known theme in Greek literature. The Christian liturgy has not only interpreted the Magnificat in terms of the birth of Jesus but has seen it time and again in the light of the death and resurrection of Jesus. In the death and resurrection of Jesus God has turned all the standards of this world upside down. It already becomes clear in the birth of Jesus that the ruler of the world is born as a poor child and that the rich go away empty. What has begun in the birth of Jesus is completed in his death and resurrection. Here the executed man becomes king and the dead man the guide to life. The light shines in darkness; the tomb becomes the place of life. With the Magnificat Luke offers the church a song which describes the mystery of Jesus in images which are at the same time images for the transformation of our own lives. As I look at Christ and at Mary I become aware of the great things that God has done for me. Thus the Magnificat becomes a personal evening prayer in which I thank God for looking today on my lowliness and doing great things in me. So this song not only mixes up past and present but at the same time mixes up Mary's experience with my personal experiences and the fate of Jesus with my own personal fate. Luke understands the art of making the past present, of combining the history of Jesus with the history of the church and our quite personal history. He has succeeded in doing that in a unique way in the Magnificat. So in this hymn, every day we celebrate God's gracious action in us in fellowship with Mary, our sister in the faith.

In Compline, the monastic night prayer, the church sings the farewell song of old Simeon. In this song, too, we encounter the ambiguity of the words. It is Simeon's song of gratitude for what he has experienced, for having seen salvation in the child in his arms, the 'light to lighten the Gentiles and glory for your people Israel' (Luke 2.32). At the same time it is our song at the end of the day. Today we have seen the salvation that God has prepared for us. Today Christ has shone for us as light, to illuminate the belief and unbelief in us. Simeon's prayer is a conversation with God at the moment of death. As we face the night, for us too it is practice in dying. The night of death has lost its terrors, because in Jesus we have seen the salvation through which our life becomes sound and whole. We have seen salvation not only in the birth of Jesus but also today, on this day. God lets us see his salvation when he touches us in silence, when he illuminates the divine mystery in our encounter with another person. Jesus' gaze opens our eyes to the salvation that is happening to us today. Because we have seen salvation today, we can confidently place ourselves in the loving arms of God tonight.

The church loves these three songs that Luke has given it. And many of the faithful like to sing these songs every day. They sense that Luke's words are full of poetry, that they are open to expressing everything that we experience today before God. They praise God for what he did in the story of Jesus then and what he is doing for us today in Jesus Christ. So Luke is present in the liturgy every day. More than almost anyone else Luke continues to influence the church. At the great festivals we hear texts from his Gospel and Acts: Christmas, Candlemas, Easter Day,

Ascension Day and Pentecost. In Advent in the days before Christmas we read Luke's Gospel above all. And at Eastertide we hear readings from the Acts of the Apostles every day. Every morning and evening we sing the songs that Luke has handed on to us. Every day they are new songs, although Luke wrote these words almost 2000 years ago. He is truly a poet who gives us the words with which we can interpret and express our life in the face of Jesus.

Conclusion

Luke has had many labels attached to him in our day: Luke the evangelist of the poor; Luke the evangelist of everyday life; Luke the evangelist of the church's year; Luke the evangelist of women; Luke the first liberation theologian. In our time the Gospel of Luke has been rediscovered above all by liberation theology and feminist theology. Protestant exegesis doesn't think much of the Gospel of Luke. There are theologians who don't believe that Luke offers any usable theology. They measure Luke by the Pauline doctrine of justification and rightly note that he puts forward a different theology from Paul. But it's good that we have not only Paul but also Luke, who brings Jesus nearer to us as a person who can tell us stories, touch our hearts and invite us to repent. More than any other evangelist, Luke speaks to women, and not just because he is the only one to report that Jesus wasn't just accompanied by the Twelve but also by some women (cf. Luke 8.2). Women were as much disciples as men. Luke touches women's hearts because he doesn't moralize but tells stories. And Luke is loved by women because he doesn't write theoretically, but always relates to his readers. He creates relationships with his writing. That gives his Gospel a different quality, a human quality.

Today Luke is as topical as he was then. He can again bring near to us this Jesus who has become a stranger to many people. Luke's picture of Jesus is inviting, fascinating. It isn't just harmonious and nice. Rather, this Jesus also shows difficult features. We have to grapple with him. We can't evade him. He provokes us with some of the things that he says. And at the same time he fascinates us by the way in which he speaks and acts. We must continue today the translation work that Luke did for the educated Greeks of his time. What is the present-day background against which we preach Jesus? How far does this background correspond to the thought-world of Hellenism? Hellenism was a conglomerate of Greek, Egyptian, Persian and Jewish influences. That has a parallel in the pluralism of our time. So our task is to translate Luke against the background of our thought. We could learn from Luke to understand the distinctive and special character of Jesus in dialogue with other religions without devaluing these religions. In particular the traditions of other religions can open our eyes to grasp the mystery of Jesus in all his depth.

Luke is modern as a theologian of social justice. The just distribution of resources will become the great political topic in the years to come. If the South and the North continue to grow apart as they are doing, the discrepancy in living conditions will lead to violent clashes. Luke's voice must be heard again today if we are to live permanently in peace. Peace isn't just an idyllic message for Christmas; steps have to be taken to secure it. And for Luke that means above all sharing possessions. We can't evade this insight of Luke's today. With good reason Luke has been called the evangelist of the poor.

Each person will have different favourite texts from the Gospel of Luke. Each person will be attracted and moved by different stories. I hope that readers will read the Gospel of Luke with new eyes, read it as they have never read it before. Perhaps they will then realize just how topical its message is. And I hope that readers will have the same experience as the disciples on the Emmaus road: 'Did not our hearts burn within us as he talked to us on the road and explained the scriptures to us?' (Luke 24.32). I hope that your hearts will burn and your eyes will be opened to understand the mystery of the merciful love of God which has shone out for us in Jesus Christ and has visited us here on earth.

The Seven Sacraments

'The sacraments are signs of how the Church actually treats such major themes as birth and death, health and sickness, growing up, love, responsibility, mission and guilt, and acts with regard to them. These are central topics addressed by all the sacraments.'

The bestselling Benedictine Fr Anselm Grün applies his extensive counselling experience, great fund of common sense, biblical insight and analytical training to the seven sacraments recognized by the Catholic Church: Baptism, Eucharist (or Communion), Confirmation, Reconciliation (Penance or Confession), Marriage, Ordination and Anointing of the Sick.

Each sacrament's meaning is examined, as well as its history, its form – past and present – and its impact on the life of those who receive it and those who administer it. Grün also suggests how the sacraments could be made more relevant to Christians living in the twenty-first century.

Everyone can benefit from reading this book: those about to receive any one of the sacraments will gain insight and inspiration; teachers, parish priests, and pastoral workers will find their work enriched and made easier; and both married and celibate will discover elements to celebrate in their own and others' way of life. As always, Grün combines flashes of radicalism with deep understanding of Catholic tradition. His is a unique voice, and here he reclaims a vital subject from widespread ignorance and neglect.

ISBN 0–8264–6704–0

Images of Jesus

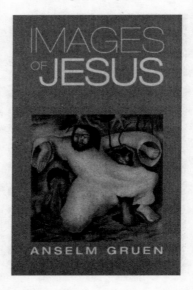

This fresh and original book about Jesus considers the Jesus of devotion, the Jesus within. It includes fifty images of Jesus, each of which provides inspiration for a meditation.

We need to get away from clichés and see what Jesus really means for people today. After a brief account of Jesus and his times, the author introduces the book and how to read it. Some of the pictures of Jesus are surprising – Jesus the drop out, the family therapist, the glutton, the vagabond and the exorcist.

ISBN 0–8264–6782–2

The Spirit of Self-Esteem

The bestselling Benedictine monk-counsellor here draws on his vast experience to make a distinctive contribution to a virtually universal problem: people's feeling of powerlessness in the face of life and the world.

'As a counsellor,' he writes, 'I have experienced the same thing again and again: a vast number of people have problems that can be traced back to a basic lack of self-esteem and to a deep-seated conviction that they are powerless and ineffectual.'

The book is divided into two parts: Acquiring Self-Esteem and Remaking the Real You. It is a work of therapy, but not one that produces merely some vague notion of self-understanding. Like Jesus in his healing mission, Grün is not afraid to move beyond understanding to confrontation. His unique combination of psychological acumen and biblical insight makes this a highly positive and deeply inspiring work for young and old, for women and men, for parents, teachers, and anyone who encounters the problem of low self-esteem in themselves and in others.

Grün writes in a contemporary idiom but always from a deep and biblically-based Catholic faith. This is a book that can make us 'take up our bed and go home' – take charge of the symptoms of our powerlessness and find our real selves, as Jesus left the paralysed man no choice but to do. This means finding God in ourselves and discovering the power of prayer and the power of love.

ISBN 0–86012–285–9

Angels of Grace

From the Angel of Love to the Angel of Quiet . . . fifty 'angels' – or virtues, or attitudes –
to inspire and help us for a week, a month, a year, a lifetime.

Angels in the Bible are messengers of God, images of God's presence. They show us that
there is 'more' to our life, that it relates to something beyond ourselves. Here, each
embodies an attitude that is a virtue, meaning, power and strength. Each is at once an
inspiration corresponding to a deep desire and the spiritual travelling companion to
give us the hope and confidence that can realize that desire. 'Angels,' says the author, 'are
here beside us, so that we are not here alone praying to God with our troubles. Angels
tell us: God is near; you are bathed in God's healing and loving presence.'

So, meet the Angel of Truthfulness, the Angel of Mercy, the Angel of Courage, the
Angel of Gratitude, the Angel of Forgiveness, the Angel of Patience, the Angel of
Freedom, and many others. They enable us to become fully what they are – and we in
fact already are – manifestations of the grace of God. All are angels of Grace.

ISBN 0–86012–283–2